WILLIAMS-SONOMA

ASIAN

RECIPES AND TEXT
FARINA WONG KINGSLEY

GENERAL EDITOR
CHUCK WILLIAMS

PHOTOGRAPHS
MAREN CARUSO

SIMON & SCHUSTER • SOURCE

NEW YORK • LONDON • TORONTO • SYDNEY • SINGAPORE

CONTENTS

RICE PLATES

NOODLE DISHES

VEGETABLE DISHES

SWEET DISHES

INTRODUCTION

Many Western cities, large and small, are home to thriving Asian communities. Visiting a Vietnamese, Korean, Japanese, or Indian restaurant in one of these locations may have been your first experience of these distinctive cuisines. Using the 40 kitchen-tested recipes in this book, you can learn to prepare such popular dishes as Japanese tempura, Thai salads, and Indian curry.

Especially if you are new to cooking Asian style, you will appreciate the detailed text in the back of the book that reviews important equipment and methods such as stir-frying, as well as the recipe side notes that cover other essential techniques and ingredients. You also can turn to the comprehensive glossary to read about Asian ingredients, so you know exactly what to seek out before you start cooking. With all these resources at your fingertips, including beautiful color photographs of the finished dishes, you will soon discover many recipes sure to become personal favorites.

Chuck Williams

THE CLASSICS

The seven time-honored favorites in this chapter represent the broad range of flavors and cooking styles found throughout Asia. From Thai noodles to Korean barbecue to Indian curry, these dishes celebrate a world of fragrant seasonings, traditional cooking methods, and distinctive national tastes, making all of them excellent choices for everyday meals.

PAD THAI

In a bowl, combine the noodles with warm water to cover and let soak for 30 minutes to rehydrate. Drain and set aside.

In a mortar, combine the chiles, shallots, and garlic and grind together with a pestle until a paste forms. Alternatively, combine the ingredients in a mini food processor and process to a paste. Set aside. Peel and devein the shrimp (page 115). Mince them and set aside.

In a wok or large, deep sauté pan over high heat, heat the canola oil until very hot. Add the chile-garlic paste and stir-fry for several seconds until fragrant. Add the fish sauce, tamarind concentrate, soy sauce, palm sugar, and lime juice and stir to combine. Add the shrimp and stir-fry just until they turn opaque, 3–5 minutes. Stir in the noodles, 1 cup (1 oz/30 g) of the bean sprouts, and the broth. Continue to cook until the noodles are tender and have absorbed all of the liquid, 5–7 minutes.

Transfer to a warmed platter. Top evenly with the omelet garnish, remaining ¼ cup (¼ oz/7 g) bean sprouts, peanuts, and cilantro. Serve at once.

Note: To make the omelet garnish, in a bowl, beat together 2 eggs, ⅛ teaspoon salt, and 1 tablespoon water. Heat a small, nonstick frying pan over medium heat and swirl in 1 teaspoon canola or peanut oil. Pour in the eggs and quickly stir for a few seconds. Stop stirring and let the omelet cook, using a spatula to lift the edges occasionally to allow the uncooked egg to flow beneath. Once the omelet is firm, after 3–4 minutes, slide it onto a cutting surface and let cool. Cut the omelet in half and then into fine julienne.

MAKES 4–6 SERVINGS

MORTAR AND PESTLE

In this Thai noodle dish, a mortar and a pestle are used to make a fragrant paste of chiles, garlic, and spices. These ancient tools are effective for pulverizing spices and other ingredients and also give the cook control over the final texture. The mortar and pestle of the Asian kitchen are stone, wood, or pottery. Mortars are bowl shaped, with a smooth or coarse-textured interior. The bat-shaped pestle is the grinding tool. To grind ingredients, place them in the mortar, then grasp the pestle and rotate and press down on the ingredients to crush them with the blunt tip.

½ lb (250 g) dried flat rice noodles, ¼ inch (6 mm) wide

2 fresh hot red chiles, seeded and chopped

2 shallots, chopped

3 cloves garlic, minced

½ lb (250 g) shrimp (prawns)

2 tablespoons canola oil

¼ cup (2 fl oz/60 ml) fish sauce

3 tablespoons tamarind concentrate (page 115)

1 tablespoon dark soy sauce

2 tablespoons chopped palm sugar (page 98)

2 tablespoons fresh lime juice

1¼ cups (1¼ oz/37 g) mung bean sprouts

½ cup (4 fl oz/125 ml) low-sodium chicken broth

Omelet garnish (see Note)

2 tablespoons unsalted peanuts, toasted (page 102) and chopped

Fresh cilantro (fresh coriander), whole sprigs or chopped, for garnish

CHICKEN SATAY WITH PEANUT DIPPING SAUCE

1½ lb (750 g) boneless, skinless chicken thighs

1½ cups (12 fl oz/375 ml) coconut milk

½ cup (4 fl oz/120 ml) fish sauce

5 tablespoons (2½ oz/ 75 g) chopped palm sugar (page 98) or brown sugar

2 tablespoons chopped fresh cilantro (fresh coriander) leaves, plus 1 tablespoon chopped stems

1 tablespoon Madras curry powder

1 shallot, chopped

2 cloves garlic

1 tablespoon *each* peeled and chopped fresh galangal (page 113) and chopped lemongrass

1 fresh hot red chile, seeded and chopped

1 tablespoon canola oil, plus oil for brushing

1 tablespoon fresh lime juice

¼ teaspoon shrimp paste (page 114)

1 cup (5 oz/155 g) unsalted peanuts, toasted (page 102) and minced

Cut the chicken into strips 4 inches (10 cm) long by 1½ inches (4 cm) wide. In a large bowl, stir together ½ cup (4 fl oz/125 ml) of the coconut milk, ¼ cup (2 fl oz/60 ml) of the fish sauce, 3 tablespoons of the palm sugar, the cilantro leaves, and the curry powder. Add the chicken strips and stir to coat evenly with the marinade. Cover and refrigerate for at least 1 hour or for up to overnight.

Prepare a hot fire in a charcoal grill, or have ready a stove-top grill pan. Place 12–15 wooden skewers, each 9 inches (23 cm) long, in water to cover and let soak for at least 20 minutes.

In a mortar, combine the shallot, garlic, galangal, lemongrass, chile, and cilantro stems and grind with a pestle, gradually adding 1–2 tablespoons water to form a paste. In a saucepan over medium heat, heat the 1 tablespoon oil. Add the shallot-garlic paste and sauté until fragrant, about 2 minutes. Stir in the remaining 1 cup (8 fl oz/250 ml) coconut milk and simmer until thickened, 7–10 minutes. Add the remaining ¼ cup (2 fl oz/60 ml) fish sauce, remaining 2 tablespoons palm sugar, lime juice, shrimp paste, and peanuts and cook until the peanut sauce thickens, 5–7 minutes.

Drain the skewers and remove the chicken strips from the marinade. Discard the marinade. Weave 3 chicken strips lengthwise onto each skewer. If using a stove-top grill pan, preheat it over high heat. Brush the grill rack or grill pan with oil. Place the skewers on the rack or pan and sear the chicken until golden brown on each side, 4–5 minutes per side. If using a charcoal grill, move the skewers away from the direct flame, cover the grill, and cook until the chicken is opaque throughout, about 5 minutes. If using a grill pan, turn off the heat, cover the pan, and let the chicken stand for about 5 minutes. Arrange the skewers on a warmed platter and serve the peanut sauce on the side.

MAKES 4 SERVINGS

COOKING WITH SKEWERS

Satay is a dish of Malaysian and Indonesian origin in which seasoned meat or seafood is woven onto skewers, grilled, and served with a sauce. Wooden, bamboo, or metal skewers may be used. Wooden or bamboo skewers need to be immersed in water for at least 20 minutes to prevent them from catching fire on the grill. Load each skewer with enough strips of marinated meat so that only the ends of the skewers are exposed. The entire length of each strip should come in contact with the grill for even cooking.

UDON WITH TOFU AND EGG

To make the braised tofu, in a saucepan, bring 4 cups (32 fl oz/1 l) water to a boil over high heat. Add the tofu, blanch for 2 minutes, and then drain. In the same saucepan over high heat, combine the stock, *mirin*, soy sauce, and sugar and bring to a boil. Add the tofu, reduce the heat to medium-low, and simmer for 5 minutes, turning the squares once at the halfway point. When the tofu turns chestnut brown, drain and cut it into thin strips. Discard the cooking liquid and set the tofu strips aside.

To make the broth, in a saucepan over high heat, combine the stock, dark and light soy sauces, vinegar, sugar, and white pepper and bring to a boil. Reduce the heat to low and keep the broth at a gentle simmer.

Bring a large saucepan three-fourths full of water to a boil over high heat. Add the salt and noodles and boil until just tender, about 2 minutes for fresh and 5 minutes for dried. Drain the noodles, rinse under running cold water, and drain again.

Divide the noodles among deep individual serving bowls. Top with the braised tofu and the green onions, dividing them evenly. Ladle the simmering broth over the noodles to cover, again dividing evenly. Carefully break an egg on top of each bowl of noodles. Garnish each serving with ¼ teaspoon of the *shichimi*.

Note: The eggs in this recipe are only partially cooked by the hot broth; see page 113 for more information.

Variation Tip: If you like, omit the tofu and eggs and serve the noodles topped with Vegetable and Shrimp Tempura (page 29).

MAKES 4 SERVINGS

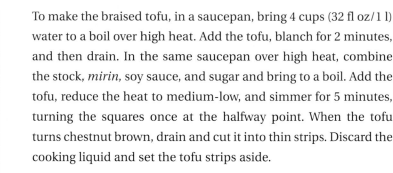

BONITO STOCK

Made from bonito flakes (page 112) and *konbu* (page 40), Japanese bonito stock, or *dashi,* is used to make soups and dipping sauces. To make the stock, wipe a ¼-lb (125-g) piece of *konbu* with a damp cloth, place in a saucepan, add 7 cups (56 fl oz/1.75 l) water, and bring to a boil over medium heat. Reduce the heat to low and simmer for 7–10 minutes. Remove the *konbu,* stir in 3½ cups (1¼ oz/37 g) bonito flakes, return to a boil, and boil for 1 minute. Strain through a fine-mesh sieve. Makes 7 cups. Instant bonito stock, in liquid form or rehydrated powder, may be substituted.

FOR THE BRAISED TOFU:

4 blocks deep-fried tofu (page 107), each 3 inches (7.5 cm) square

1 cup (8 fl oz/250 ml) bonito stock *(far left)*

1 tablespoon *mirin* **or Chinese rice wine**

1 tablespoon dark soy sauce

1 tablespoon sugar

FOR THE BROTH:

6 cups (48 fl oz/1.5 l) bonito stock *(far left)*

2 tablespoons dark soy sauce

2 tablespoons light soy sauce

1 tablespoon rice vinegar

1 tablespoon sugar

⅛ teaspoon white pepper

1 teaspoon salt

¾ lb (375 g) fresh or dried udon noodles

4 green (spring) onions, including tender green tops, julienned

4 large eggs

1 teaspoon *shichimi* **(page 114)**

POT STICKERS

¼ cup (¼ oz/7 g) dried
shiitake mushrooms

2 cups (6 oz/185 g) finely
chopped napa cabbage

½ teaspoon salt

¼ lb (125 g) ground
(minced) pork

½ cup (¾ oz/20 g) minced
fresh garlic chives (page 75)

1 tablespoon *each* light
soy sauce and Asian
sesame oil

1½ teaspoons Chinese
rice wine

1½ teaspoons peeled and
minced fresh ginger

1 clove garlic, minced

1½ tablespoons
cornstarch (cornflour)

⅛ teaspoon ground
white pepper

45 thin, round wonton
wrappers

4 tablespoons (2 fl oz/
60 ml) canola or peanut oil

1 cup (8 fl oz/250 ml)
low-sodium chicken broth

Ginger-Soy Dipping Sauce
(page 110)

Soak the dried mushrooms in warm water to cover for 30 minutes (page 30). Drain, remove the stems, and mince the caps.

In a large bowl, toss together the cabbage and salt and let stand for 30 minutes to leach out water from the cabbage. Using your hands, wring out as much of the water from the cabbage as possible. Discard the water and place the cabbage in a clean bowl. Add the mushrooms, pork, garlic chives, soy sauce, sesame oil, rice wine, ginger, garlic, cornstarch, and white pepper and, using a rubber spatula, mix vigorously to combine the ingredients well.

To fill each pot sticker, place a wonton wrapper on a work surface and brush the edges with water; keep the other wrappers covered with a slightly damp kitchen towel to prevent them from drying out. Place 1 teaspoon filling in the center of the wrapper, fold the wrapper in half to enclose the filling, and pleat the outer edge (*right*). Place the finished pot sticker on a lightly floured baking sheet. Repeat with the remaining filling and wrappers.

Preheat the oven to 250°F (120°C). In a large nonstick frying pan over medium-high heat, heat 1 tablespoon of the canola oil. Add 10–12 pot stickers, flat bottom down and in a single layer. Sear until golden brown on the bottom, 3–4 minutes. Pour ¼ cup (2 fl oz/60 ml) of the broth into the pan, cover, and let steam until all the broth evaporates, the pot stickers are tender but still firm, and the filling is cooked through, 4–5 minutes. Transfer to a platter, cover with aluminum foil, and keep warm in the oven. Cook the remaining pot stickers and broth in 3 more batches.

Serve the pot stickers hot, accompanied with the dipping sauce.

MAKES 40–45 POT STICKERS

PLEATING POT STICKERS

Traditionally eaten as a snack or an appetizer, these Chinese panfried dumplings call for thin, 3-inch (7.5-cm) round wonton wrappers. To pleat a filled pot sticker, after folding the wonton wrapper into a half-moon, pinch the edges together at one end of the arc. Then, using your thumb and index finger, and starting from the sealed end, make 4 or 5 pleats, or tucks, along the arc to enclose the filling completely. As each dumpling is formed, press the bottom lightly against your palm to flatten it slightly.

BEEF AND BROCCOLI WITH OYSTER SAUCE

Cut the steak across the grain into strips 3 inches (7.5 cm) long and ¼ inch (6 mm) thick. In a bowl, stir together the cornstarch, salt, sugar, baking soda, and 2 tablespoons water. Add the beef and stir until well mixed. Let stand at room temperature for 30 minutes.

Meanwhile, make the sauce. In a bowl, combine the oyster sauce, dark and light soy sauces, peanut oil, cornstarch, sugar, white pepper, and 2 tablespoons water. Set aside.

Bring a saucepan three-fourths full of water to a boil, add the broccoli florets, and blanch until just tender, 3–4 minutes. Drain, rinse under running cold water until cool, and then drain again. Set aside.

Remove the beef from the bowl and pat dry with paper towels. In a wok or large, deep sauté pan over high heat, heat 2 tablespoons of the peanut oil until very hot. Add the beef and stir-fry until it just turns opaque, about 3–4 minutes. Using a slotted spoon, quickly transfer the beef to a sieve placed over a bowl to drain.

Wipe out the pan with paper towels, and reheat over high heat. Add the remaining 1 tablespoon oil and heat until very hot. Add the garlic and ginger and stir-fry just until golden brown, 15–20 seconds. Using the slotted spoon, lift out the garlic and ginger and discard. Add the onion to the pan and stir-fry until just tender, about 5 minutes. Pour in the rice wine and deglaze the pan, stirring to dislodge any browned bits from the bottom. When the wine has evaporated, add the sauce, stir, and bring to a boil. Immediately add the beef and broccoli and stir-fry until the sauce thickens and the beef is heated through, about 3 minutes. Transfer the beef and broccoli to a warmed bowl and serve.

MAKES 4–6 SERVINGS

OYSTER SAUCE

This concentrated dark brown sauce with a slightly sweet, smoky flavor is made from dried oysters, salt, and water, with cornstarch (cornflour) and caramel added for consistency and color. The sauce originated in southern China, where cooks use it as a seasoning, drizzling it over simply cooked vegetables or mixing it into a meat and vegetable stir-fry. Oyster sauce also can be served as a dipping sauce for roasted meats. Avoid the least expensive products, as they lack a rich oyster flavor. Once opened, oyster sauce should be stored in the refrigerator.

1 lb (500 g) flank steak

1 tablespoon cornstarch (cornflour)

¼ teaspoon *each* salt and sugar

⅛ teaspoon baking soda (bicarbonate of soda)

FOR THE SAUCE:

2 tablespoons oyster sauce

1 tablespoon *each* dark soy sauce and light soy sauce

1 teaspoon peanut oil

1 teaspoon cornstarch (cornflour)

½ teaspoon sugar

⅛ teaspoon white pepper

2 cups (4 oz/125 g) small broccoli florets

3 tablespoons peanut oil

2 cloves garlic

2 slices fresh ginger, smashed with the side of a knife

1 small yellow onion, cut into 1-inch (2.5-cm) dice

1 tablespoon Chinese rice wine

INDIAN CHICKEN CURRY

2 teaspoons *each* coriander seeds and cumin seeds

1 teaspoon salt

1 teaspoon ground turmeric

½ teaspoon ground black pepper

⅛ teaspoon cayenne pepper

2 tablespoons canola oil

1 lb (500 g) boneless, skinless chicken thighs

¼ cup (1½ oz/45 g) unsalted cashews

1 large yellow onion

2 small tomatoes

2 tablespoons clarified butter (page 112) or canola oil

3 cloves garlic, minced

1 tablespoon peeled and minced fresh ginger

1 teaspoon seeded and minced green jalapeño chile

2 *each* bay leaves and star anise

½ cup (4 fl oz/125 ml) coconut milk

1 tablespoon fresh lemon juice

1 tablespoon chopped fresh cilantro (fresh coriander)

Toast and grind the coriander and cumin seeds *(right)*. In a bowl, stir together the toasted seeds, ½ teaspoon of the salt, and the turmeric, black pepper, cayenne pepper, and canola oil until well mixed. Cut the chicken into 1-inch (2.5-cm) cubes. Add to the bowl and stir to coat evenly. Cover and refrigerate for at least 1 hour or up to overnight.

Toast the cashews (page 102) and then chop coarsely. Set aside.

Thinly slice the onion. Cut the tomatoes in half crosswise and remove the seeds, then chop the flesh. In a sauté pan over high heat, heat the clarified butter. Add the onion and sauté until it begins to soften, 3–4 minutes. Add the garlic, ginger, chile, bay leaves, and star anise and continue to sauté until the onion is light golden brown, 5–7 minutes. Add the chicken and sauté just until the meat turns opaque, about 5 minutes. Add the tomatoes and cook, stirring occasionally, until they soften, about 2 minutes.

Stir in the coconut milk and remaining ½ teaspoon salt and bring to a gentle boil. Reduce the heat to low, cover, and simmer until the chicken is tender, about 20 minutes. Stir in the lemon juice and simmer for 5 minutes longer.

Transfer to a warmed bowl, garnish with the cashews and cilantro, and serve.

Serving Tip: Offer basmati rice to accompany the chicken and its curry sauce.

MAKES 4–6 SERVINGS

TOASTING SPICES AND SEEDS

Spices and seeds are heated in a dry pan to release their full flavor before using them in curries and other dishes. Toast spices like cumin and coriander seeds over medium-high heat until the seeds begin to pop, 2–3 minutes. Sesame seeds, with their higher oil content, should be toasted over medium heat until golden brown, 4–5 minutes. In all cases, shake the pan for even toasting. Use a spice grinder or a coffee mill reserved for spices to grind toasted spices into a powder; use a mortar and pestle for grinding sesame seeds.

KOREAN BARBECUED BEEF

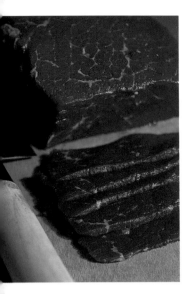

THIN-SLICING MEAT

Korean cooks slice beef for grilling very thinly to allow for quick marinating and only the briefest cooking. A sharp chef's knife is key to slicing the meat sufficiently thin. For easier slicing, first place the beef in the freezer just until firm, 20–30 minutes. Then, using a single deliberate motion, slice the meat across the grain ⅛ inch (3 mm) thick. Avoid sawing the meat, which results in slices with jagged edges. If the slices are too thick, place them between sheets of parchment (baking) or waxed paper and pound to an even ⅛-inch thickness with a meat pounder.

Cut the beef across the grain into slices ⅛ inch (3 mm) thick *(left)*. Working on a cutting board, use the side of the blade of a chef's knife or cleaver to mash together three-fourths of the chopped garlic and the 1 tablespoon sugar, forming a paste. Place the paste in a bowl and stir in 3 tablespoons of the light soy sauce, the dark soy sauce, the 1 tablespoon sesame oil, 1 tablespoon of the vinegar, all but 1 tablespoon of the minced green onions, the ginger, 1 tablespoon of the sesame seeds, the black pepper, and 1 tablespoon water. Place the beef in a shallow bowl and pour the marinade on top. Mix well, cover, and refrigerate for 1–3 hours.

Meanwhile, make a dipping sauce. On a cutting board, use the side of the blade of a chef's knife or cleaver to mash together the remaining chopped garlic and ½ teaspoon sugar, forming a paste. Place the paste in a bowl and whisk in the remaining 3 tablespoons soy sauce, the remaining 1 tablespoon vinegar, the chile sauce, the remaining 1 teaspoon sesame oil, the reserved 1 tablespoon minced green onions, the remaining 1 tablespoon sesame seeds, and 1 tablespoon water. Set aside until ready to serve.

Prepare a hot fire in a charcoal grill, or preheat a stove-top grill pan over high heat.

Brush the grill rack or pan with the canola oil. Remove the beef from the marinade and pat dry. Discard the marinade. Working in batches, arrange in a single layer on the rack or pan. Sear, turning once, until crisp and brown on both sides, about 2 minutes per side. Wipe and oil the rack or pan between batches if necessary.

Transfer to a warmed platter, garnish with the shredded green onion, and serve at once with the dipping sauce.

Serving Tip: The beef can be served on red-leaf lettuce leaves with rice (page 61), kimchi *(page 113), and a drizzling of dipping sauce.*

MAKES 4–6 SERVINGS

1½ lb (750 g) beef tenderloin, about 5 inches (13 cm) thick

4 cloves garlic, chopped

1 tablespoon plus ½ teaspoon sugar

6 tablespoons (3 fl oz/ 90 ml) light soy sauce

1 tablespoon dark soy sauce

1 tablespoon plus 1 teaspoon Asian sesame oil

2 tablespoons rice vinegar

5 green (spring) onions, minced, plus shredded green onion for garnish

1 teaspoon peeled and grated fresh ginger

2 tablespoons sesame seeds, toasted (page 21) and crushed

½ teaspoon ground black pepper

1 teaspoon Sriracha chile sauce (page 115)

1 tablespoon canola oil

SMALL PLATES

Adapted from the ubiquitous street foods of Asia, many of these appetizing small dishes are eaten as satisfying afternoon—or sometimes late-night—snacks in their countries of origin. Yet all of them, from delicate Vietnamese rolls filled with vegetables and rice noodles to a salad pairing beef and mango, translate easily into wonderful starters for nearly any meal.

VIETNAMESE SUMMER ROLLS
26

VEGETABLE AND SHRIMP TEMPURA
29

MINCED CHICKEN IN LETTUCE CUPS
30

VEGETABLE SAMOSAS
33

THAI BEEF SALAD WITH MANGO
34

MUNG BEAN CRÊPES
37

VIETNAMESE SUMMER ROLLS

RICE PAPER

Thin, brittle sheets made from rice flour and water, rice paper is used primarily in Vietnamese cuisine for making fried rolls or fresh rolls like the ones here. To prepare the rice paper for use, fill a wide, shallow bowl with warm water. One at a time, slip a round of rice paper into the water, letting it sit for 2–3 minutes until soft. While the rice paper is still in the water, massage it with your fingers until it is pliable, about 1 minute. Remove the sheet from the water, lay it on a damp kitchen towel, and use as directed in the recipe.

Working with 1 rice-paper round at a time, soak the round in warm water *(left)*.

To assemble each roll, lay a lettuce leaf horizontally on the bottom half of the moistened rice paper. At the base of the lettuce, place several strands of noodles, 1 teaspoon each of the carrot and cucumber, 2 slices tofu, 1 tablespoon of the bean sprouts, and several leaves of mint and cilantro. Be careful not to overstuff the rolls. Lift the bottom edge of the rice paper and carefully place over the noodles and other ingredients, then roll once to form a tight cylinder. Fold in the sides of the rice paper and continue to roll the rice paper and filling into a cylinder.

Place the prepared rolls, seam side down, on a platter and cover with a damp kitchen towel. The rolls can be held at room temperature for several hours before serving.

Just before serving, cut each roll in half at an angle. Serve with Nuoc Cham.

Note: Traditionally, the term spring rolls *has been used to describe both rolls that are fried after filling and rolls that are served without further cooking. The term* summer roll *has come to refer to an uncooked roll made with noodles, fresh vegetables and herbs, and other ingredients.*

MAKES 4–6 SERVINGS

8 rice-paper rounds, each 12 inches (30 cm) in diameter

8 red-leaf lettuce leaves, stems removed

2 oz (60 g) cellophane noodles, soaked in warm water for 15 minutes and drained

1 carrot, peeled and finely shredded

½ small cucumber, peeled and seeded (page 113), then finely shredded

½-lb (250-g) block extra-firm tofu, cut into 16 slices each 4 inches (10 cm) long by ¼ inch (6 mm) thick

½ cup (½ oz/15 g) mung bean sprouts

Leaves from 1 bunch fresh mint

Leaves from 1 bunch fresh cilantro (fresh coriander)

Nuoc Cham (page 111) for serving

VEGETABLE AND SHRIMP TEMPURA

1 carrot, peeled

1 small sweet potato, peeled

1 small yellow onion

2 oz (60 g) green beans, trimmed

1 zucchini (courgette)

5 fresh shiitake mushrooms, about 1½ inches (4 cm) in diameter, stems removed

Canola or peanut oil for deep-frying

1 cup (4 oz/125 g) cake (soft-wheat) flour

1 cup (4 oz/125 g) rice flour

¾ teaspoon salt

¼ teaspoon baking soda (bicarbonate of soda)

2 large egg yolks

1½ cups (12 fl oz/375 ml) ice water

8 large shrimp (prawns), peeled and deveined (page 115)

Tempura Dipping Sauce (far right)

Cut the carrot into pieces 5 inches (13 cm) long and ¼ inch (6 mm) thick. Using as much of the sweet potato as needed to yield ½ cup (2½ oz/75 g), cut into slices ⅛ inch (3 mm) thick, and then cut each slice in half to form half-moons. Cut the onion into slices ½ inch (12 mm) thick. Cut the green beans into 5-inch (13-cm) lengths. Cut the zucchini into pieces 5 inches (13 cm) long and ¼ inch (6 mm) thick. Cut the mushroom caps in half.

Preheat the oven to 250°F (120°C). Pour oil to a depth of 5 inches (13 cm) into a wok or deep saucepan and heat to 370°F (188°C) on a deep-frying thermometer. Line a baking sheet with a double thickness of paper towels.

Meanwhile, in a bowl, sift together the cake and rice flours, salt, and baking soda. In a small bowl, using a fork, beat together the egg yolks and ice water. Stir the egg-water mixture into the flour mixture just until the batter comes together.

Working in small batches, dip the vegetables into the batter, allowing any excess to drip off, and then slip them into the hot oil. Deep-fry until light golden brown, 1–2 minutes. Using a wire skimmer, transfer the vegetables to the paper towels to drain. Transfer to an ovenproof platter and place in the oven. Between batches, use the skimmer to remove any batter bits from the oil.

Before dipping the shrimp in the batter, make several slashes in the underside (concave side) of each shrimp to prevent curling while frying. Reheat the oil to 370°F (188°C) and, working in batches, dip the shrimp into the batter, allowing any excess to drip off, and then slip them into the hot oil. Deep-fry until light golden brown, 30–60 seconds. Using the skimmer, transfer the shrimp to the platter with the vegetables.

Serve the tempura with the dipping sauce.

MAKES 4 SERVINGS

TEMPURA DIPPING SAUCE

An iconic dish of Japan, tempura was introduced to the island nation by missionaries from Portugal in the sixteenth century. The Japanese refined this foreign dish, serving it with a dipping sauce. To make the sauce, in a saucepan, combine ½ cup (4 fl oz/125 ml) bonito stock (page 14), 3 tablespoons *each* dark soy and *mirin* (or Chinese rice wine), and ½ teaspoon sugar. Bring to a boil, add 1 heaping tablespoon bonito flakes (page 112), and then strain through a fine-mesh sieve. Serve the sauce at room temperature. Makes 1 cup (8 fl oz/250 ml).

MINCED CHICKEN IN LETTUCE CUPS

DRIED MUSHROOMS

The rich, earthy flavor of mushrooms intensifies when they are dried, resulting in a distinct flavor essential to many Asian braised and stir-fried preparations, including this classic Chinese dish. Dried Chinese black mushrooms, also marketed as dried shiitakes, are the type most frequently used. Before using dried mushrooms, rinse them and place in a bowl of boiling water, keeping them submerged with a lid or plate. Let soak for 30 minutes, then remove from the water and trim off the tough stems. Strain the soaking liquid if using in the recipe.

Cut out the stem from the base of the lettuce and discard. Immerse the lettuce head in a large bowl of very cold water and let soak for 30 minutes. Remove from the water and separate 20 leaves, reserving the remaining lettuce for another use. Trim each leaf into a palm-sized cup. Refrigerate the lettuce cups until ready to assemble. Meanwhile, soak the mushrooms *(left)* and then mince and set aside.

In a small bowl, stir together the oyster sauce, dark and light soy sauces, sesame oil, sugar, cornstarch, white pepper, and egg until well mixed. Set aside.

In a wok or large, deep sauté pan over high heat, heat the canola oil until very hot. Add the ginger and garlic and stir-fry until light golden brown, 15–20 seconds. Add the chicken and pork and stir-fry until the meat turns opaque, 5–7 minutes. Pour off any liquid that has collected in the bottom of the pan.

Return the pan to high heat, add the bamboo shoots, water chestnuts, and mushrooms, and stir-fry until any moisture has evaporated, 3–4 minutes. Stir in the oyster sauce mixture and continue to stir-fry until the sauce thickens, about 5 minutes. Remove from the heat.

In a measuring cup, mix the hoisin sauce with 1 tablespoon warm water. Thinly slice the green onions on the diagonal. Arrange the lettuce cups on a large platter. Spoon a heaping tablespoon of the hot chicken mixture into each lettuce cup, drizzle with a little hoisin sauce, and top with the green onions and pine nuts, dividing evenly. Serve at once.

MAKES 5 SERVINGS

1 large head iceberg lettuce

6 dried Chinese black mushrooms

2 tablespoons oyster sauce

1 tablespoon *each* dark soy sauce and light soy sauce

1 teaspoon Asian sesame oil

½ teaspoon *each* sugar and cornstarch (cornflour)

⅛ teaspoon ground white pepper

1 large egg, beaten

2 tablespoons canola oil

1 tablespoon peeled and minced fresh ginger

2 cloves garlic, minced

½ lb (250 g) chicken thigh meat, minced

¼ lb (125 g) ground (minced) pork

½ cup (2 oz/60 g) minced canned bamboo shoots

6 canned water chestnuts, minced

¼ cup (2 fl oz/60 ml) hoisin sauce

3 green (spring) onions

2 tablespoons pine nuts, toasted (page 102)

VEGETABLE SAMOSAS

2 boiling potatoes,
1 lb (500 g) total weight,
peeled

¼ cup (1½ oz/45 g) diced
carrots (¼-inch/6-mm dice)

¼ cup (1½ oz/45 g) fresh
or thawed frozen English
peas

1 yellow onion, chopped

3 cloves garlic

1 tablespoon peeled and
chopped fresh ginger

2 tablespoons canola or
peanut oil, plus oil for
deep-frying

1 teaspoon ground
turmeric

½ teaspoon *each* ground
coriander, ground cumin,
and sugar

¾ teaspoon salt, plus salt
to taste

⅛ teaspoon ground black
pepper, plus pepper to
taste

1 green jalapeño chile,
seeded and minced

1 tablespoon all-purpose
(plain) flour

12 spring-roll wrappers

Cilantro and Mint Chutney
(page 111) or Tamarind
Chutney (page 111)

In a saucepan over high heat, combine the potatoes with water to cover generously. Bring to a boil and cook until just tender, about 15 minutes. Drain, let cool, peel, and cut into ¼-inch (6-mm) dice. Fill a small saucepan three-fourths full of water, bring to a boil, add the carrots, and blanch for 2 minutes. Using a skimmer, lift out and set aside. Add the peas to the boiling water, blanch for 3 minutes, drain, and set aside.

In a mini food processor, combine the onion, garlic, ginger, and 2 tablespoons water and process to a paste. In a large sauté pan over high heat, heat the 2 tablespoons canola oil. Add the onion mixture and sauté until light golden brown, 5–7 minutes. Reduce the heat to medium-low and add the turmeric, coriander, cumin, sugar, ¾ teaspoon salt, ⅛ teaspoon pepper, and chile and cook for 2 minutes to blend the flavors. Stir in the blanched carrots and peas and sauté until most of the moisture has evaporated, 3–4 minutes. Stir in the diced potatoes. Taste and adjust the seasoning with salt and pepper. Transfer to a plate and let cool.

In a small bowl, stir together the flour and ¼ cup (2 fl oz/60 ml) water to form a thin paste. Separate the spring-roll wrappers and cover with a damp kitchen towel. Working with 1 wrapper at a time, cut it in half to form 2 rectangles. Use each half to enclose 1 tablespoon of the filling *(right)*.

Preheat the oven to 250°F (120°C). Pour oil to a depth of 5 inches (13 cm) into a deep frying pan and heat to 370°F (188°C) on a deep-frying thermometer. Working in batches of 3 or 4 samosas, carefully lower them into the oil and deep-fry until golden brown, 2–3 minutes. Using a wire skimmer, transfer to paper towels to drain. Allow the oil to reheat to 370°F between batches. Place the fried samosas on an ovenproof platter and keep warm in the oven as you cook the remaining batches. Serve with chutney.

MAKES 6 SERVINGS

FOLDING SAMOSAS

These popular Indian snacks are traditionally made with a handmade flour-and-shortening dough. Spring-roll wrappers are an easy, lighter substitute. To fold a samosa, with a short side of 1 rectangle facing you, place 2 teaspoons filling on the lower left corner. Fold the lower right corner over the filling to form a triangle. Bring the bottom left corner of the triangle up against the straight edge, again forming a triangle. Fold again on the diagonal, aligning the left edge with the right edge. Repeat until only a small border remains, then seal the edge with a water-flour paste.

THAI BEEF SALAD WITH MANGO

In a large bowl, stir together the coconut milk, ¼ cup fish sauce, minced garlic, 2 tablespoons palm sugar, and minced cilantro until well mixed. Add the flank steak and turn to coat well. Cover and marinate at room temperature for 1 hour.

Seed and finely chop each jalapeño chile. In a mortar, combine the chiles, chopped garlic, chopped cilantro stems and mint, and pepper and grind together with a pestle until a paste forms. Transfer the paste to a large bowl and whisk in the ⅓ cup fish sauce, lime juice, and 1 teaspoon palm sugar. Drizzle in the canola oil while continuously whisking. Cover the dressing and refrigerate until ready to dress the salad.

Peel the mangoes and cut the flesh into thin slices (page 114). Using only the bulb of the lemongrass stalk, peel away the tough outer layer, smash the stalk with the side of a chef's knife, and cut on the diagonal into ⅛-inch (3-mm) slices. Seed and julienne the red chile. Set aside.

Preheat the oven to 400°F (200°C). Prepare a hot fire in a charcoal grill, or preheat a stove-top grill pan over high heat.

Remove the steak from the marinade and pat dry with paper towels. Discard the marinade. Place on the grill rack or grill pan and sear, turning once, until brown on both sides, 5–6 minutes per side. Using tongs, transfer the steak to a rimmed baking sheet, place in the oven, and cook for 5 minutes longer for rare and 10 minutes for medium. Transfer the steak to a cutting board and let rest for 5 minutes. Slice across the grain into thin strips. Pour the juices released during slicing into the dressing, stir well, then add the beef, mangoes, lemongrass, red chile, shallots, and julienned herbs. Toss to coat. Line a serving platter with lettuce leaves, spoon the beef mixture on top, and serve.

MAKES 4–6 SERVINGS

1 cup (8 fl oz/250 ml) coconut milk

¼ cup (2 fl oz/60 ml) plus ⅓ cup (3 fl oz/80 ml) fish sauce

3 cloves garlic, minced, plus 3 cloves, chopped

2 tablespoons plus 1 teaspoon finely chopped palm sugar (page 98) or brown sugar

1 tablespoon minced fresh cilantro (fresh coriander)

1 lb (500 g) flank steak

2 green jalapeño chiles

2 tablespoons *each* chopped fresh cilantro (fresh coriander) stems and chopped fresh mint

⅛ teaspoon ground black pepper

5 tablespoons (2½ fl oz/75 ml) fresh lime juice

2 tablespoons canola oil

2 mangoes

1 *each* lemongrass stalk and fresh hot red chile

2 shallots, thinly sliced

¼ cup (⅓ oz/10 g) *each* julienned fresh Thai basil, fresh mint leaves, and fresh cilantro (fresh coriander)

1 head red-leaf lettuce

MUNG BEAN CRÊPES

½ cup (3½ oz/105 g) dried yellow mung beans

1½ cups (12 fl oz/375 ml) coconut milk

¾ cup (4 oz/125 g) rice flour

2½ teaspoons sugar

½ teaspoon *each* salt and ground turmeric

1 lb (500 g) shrimp (prawns), peeled and deveined (page 115)

2½ tablespoons fish sauce

3 cloves garlic, minced

¼ teaspoon ground black pepper

1 large yellow onion

10 fresh button mushrooms

5 tablespoons (3 fl oz/ 80 ml) canola oil, or as needed

2 cups (2 oz/60 g) mung bean sprouts

1 head red-leaf lettuce, leaves separated

½ cup (½ oz/15 g) *each* fresh mint sprigs, fresh cilantro (fresh coriander) sprigs, and fresh Thai basil leaves

Nuoc Cham (page 111)

Soak the mung beans *(right)*. In a blender, combine the soaked beans and coconut milk. Purée until smooth. Add the rice flour, 1½ teaspoons of the sugar, the salt, and the turmeric. Process until well mixed. Pour the mung bean batter through a fine-mesh sieve placed over a bowl, cover, and refrigerate until ready to use. In a bowl, combine the shrimp, fish sauce, garlic, remaining 1 teaspoon sugar, and pepper, stir well, and let stand for 30 minutes.

Thinly slice the onion. Remove the stems from the mushrooms and thinly slice the caps. In a large sauté pan over high heat, heat 2 tablespoons of the canola oil. Add the onion and sauté until light golden brown, 4–5 minutes. Add the mushrooms and sauté until they begin to wilt, about 5 minutes. Transfer to a bowl and add the bean sprouts to the bowl. Wipe the pan with paper towels, return it to high heat, and heat 1 tablespoon canola oil. Add the shrimp and their marinade and sauté until they turn opaque and are cooked through, about 5 minutes. Add to the mushroom mixture.

In a nonstick 10-inch (25-cm) frying pan over medium heat, heat 2 tablespoons canola oil. When the oil is hot, pour in ¼ cup (2 fl oz/ 60 ml) batter and quickly swirl to cover the pan bottom evenly. Cook until crisp and brown at the edges and set in the middle, 5–7 minutes. Remove from the heat and, using a wide spatula, slide the crêpe, crisp side down, onto a platter. Spread 3 heaping tablespoons of the mushroom mixture onto half of the crêpe. Carefully fold the crêpe over the filling. Repeat to make 3 or 4 more crêpes, adding more oil to the pan if needed and evenly distributing the shrimp among the crêpes.

Arrange the lettuce and herbs on plates. The crêpes are cut in half, and diners wrap each half with lettuce, garnish with fresh herbs, and drizzle with Nuoc Cham.

MAKES 8–10 SERVINGS

MUNG BEANS

Mung beans turn up in various guises in Asian cooking, with fresh sprouts being the most common form. This favorite dish of southern Vietnam uses yellow mung beans—split dried green mung beans with their husks removed. Before using the dried beans, pick through them, discarding any misshapen beans or grit, rinse, put in a bowl, and add boiling water. Let soak for 30 minutes, and then drain.

SOUPS

Soup in Asia plays two basic roles—as part of a meal, usually broth with a few ingredients, or as a meal in itself, often including noodles and meat or seafood. Japanese miso soup with bits of tofu and seaweed will fit easily into a dinner menu, while Malaysian curry noodle soup or Indonesian chicken noodle soup alone will satisfy even the heartiest eater.

MISO SOUP WITH TOFU AND SEAWEED
40

MALAYSIAN COCONUT CURRY SOUP
43

VIETNAMESE BEEF NOODLE SOUP
44

SPICY TOFU AND BAMBOO SHOOT SOUP
47

INDONESIAN SPICY CHICKEN NOODLE SOUP
48

THAI SHRIMP AND LEMONGRASS SOUP
51

MISO SOUP WITH TOFU AND SEAWEED

KONBU

This type of dried sea kelp gathered mainly off the northern Japanese island of Hokkaido is fundamental to Japanese cuisine. Usually sold in small squares, *konbu* is a dark olive green covered with a white salt residue, and has a strong "seafood" taste and fragrance. Its most common use is as a flavoring for bonito stock (page 14), but it is also added to soups and stir-fries. Never rinse it under running water, as some of its flavor will be lost; instead, wipe it lightly with a damp cloth. When rehydrated, *konbu* expands and takes on a crunchy texture.

If using the *konbu,* soak in just enough hot water to cover until soft, about 20 minutes. If using *wakame,* soak in hot water to cover until soft, about 10 minutes. Drain and cut into strips 4 inches (10 cm) long by ⅛ inch (3 mm) wide. Set aside.

Bring a small saucepan three-fourths full of water to a gentle boil over medium heat. Add the tofu block, reduce the heat to low, and simmer for 5 minutes to firm up the tofu. Carefully drain the tofu, place on a salad plate, and top with a second plate. The sandwiched plates act as a weight to force out excess water from the tofu. Set aside for 30 minutes. Just before preparing the soup, pour off any water and carefully cut the tofu into ½-inch (12-mm) cubes.

In a large saucepan over low heat, bring the stock to a bare simmer. Whisk in the miso paste, *mirin,* vinegar, and sesame oil. Simmer for 5 minutes. Stir in the *konbu* or *wakame* and the mushrooms, and then gently add the tofu cubes and green onions. Season the soup with the white pepper and salt. Do not allow the soup to boil, or the tofu will break apart.

Ladle the soup into warmed bowls and serve at once.

Note: Wakame *is a variety of seaweed with green curly leaves. The dried leaves, sold in small packages, are reconstituted briefly before use in a recipe.*

MAKES 4–6 SERVINGS

3 oz (90 g) *konbu (far left)* or *wakame* (see Note), wiped with a damp cloth

3-by-3-by-5-inch (7.5-by-7.5-by-13-cm) block soft tofu

6 cups (48 fl oz/1.5 l) bonito stock (page 14) or low-sodium chicken broth

6 tablespoons (3 oz/90 g) white miso paste (page 115)

1 tablespoon *mirin* or Chinese rice wine

1 teaspoon rice vinegar

½ teaspoon Asian sesame oil

2 oz (60 g) enoki mushrooms, stems trimmed

3 green (spring) onions, thinly sliced on the diagonal

¼ teaspoon ground white pepper

⅛ teaspoon salt

MALAYSIAN COCONUT CURRY SOUP

3 tablespoons canola oil

Chile paste (far right)

3 cups (24 fl oz/750 ml) coconut milk

¼ cup (2 fl oz/60 ml) fish sauce

2 tablespoons *each* fresh lime juice and chopped palm sugar (page 98)

1 tablespoon tamarind concentrate (page 115)

½ lb (250 g) large shrimp (prawns)

½ lb (250 g) cleaned squid

12 mussels

2 green (spring) onions

1 teaspoon salt

1 lb (500 g) fresh thin round Chinese egg noodles

1 green jalapeño chile, seeded and thinly sliced on the diagonal

Omelet garnish (see Note, page 10)

1 cup (1 oz/30 g) mung bean sprouts

¼ cup (¼ oz/7 g) *each* fresh Thai basil sprigs and fresh cilantro (fresh coriander) sprigs

1 lime, cut into wedges

In a large saucepan over high heat, heat the canola oil. Add the chile paste and sauté until fragrant, about 2 minutes. Add the coconut milk, fish sauce, lime juice, palm sugar, tamarind concentrate, and 2 cups (16 fl oz/500 ml) water and bring to a gentle boil. Boil for 2 minutes, then reduce the heat to low and simmer for 10 minutes to blend the flavors.

Meanwhile, peel and devein the shrimp (page 115). Cut the squid crosswise into rings 1 inch (2.5 cm) wide. Scrub the mussels well and remove any beards. Thinly slice the green onions on the diagonal. Set aside.

Bring a large saucepan three-fourths full of water to a boil. Add the salt and the noodles and boil until the noodles are just tender, 2–3 minutes. Using a wire skimmer, remove the noodles from the water and divide evenly among warmed individual bowls. Add the shrimp to the same boiling water, reduce the heat to medium, and poach the shrimp until they just turn opaque, about 1 minute. Lift out with the skimmer and place in a bowl.

Add the squid to the same simmering water and cook just until they curl and turn opaque, about 1 minute. Lift out and add to the bowl holding the shrimp. Then add the mussels, discarding any that fail to close to the touch, to the simmering water and cook until they open, 2–3 minutes. Lift out, discarding any that failed to open, and add to the seafood. Discard the water.

Divide the seafood evenly among the bowls holding the noodles. Ladle the hot coconut curry broth over the seafood, dividing it evenly. Divide the green onions, chile slices, omelet garnish, bean sprouts, herb sprigs, and lime wedges evenly among the bowls. Serve at once.

MAKES 4–6 SERVINGS

MALAYSIAN CHILE PASTE

Giving this Malaysian soup its depth of flavor is a freshly made chile paste. To make the paste, in a mortar, combine 3 shallots, chopped; 2 fresh hot red chiles, seeded and chopped; 2 cloves garlic, chopped; 1 lemongrass stalk, bulb only, chopped; 1 table-spoon chopped galangal (page 113); 1 tablespoon chopped fresh cilantro (fresh coriander) stems; 1 teaspoon ground turmeric; and ½ tea-spoon shrimp paste (page 114). Grind together with a pestle until a paste forms, adding 1 tablespoon water if needed to facilitate blending.

VIETNAMESE BEEF NOODLE SOUP

GARNISHES

Making this recipe for *pho*, the classic beef noodle soup of Hanoi, begins with preparing a well-seasoned broth, which is then ladled over rice vermicelli, thin slices of beef, and a selection of vegetables. Raw vegetables and other garnishes are offered at the table as a flavor and texture contrast. To serve the garnishes, arrange on a platter 2 cups (2 oz/60 g) mung bean sprouts; 2 green jalapeño chiles, seeded and thinly sliced on the diagonal; 2 limes, cut into wedges; and ½ cup (½ oz/15 g) *each* small fresh mint sprigs, fresh Thai basil sprigs, and fresh cilantro (fresh coriander) sprigs.

Preheat the oven to 450°F (230°C). In a large roasting pan, place the beef bones in a single layer. Roast for 15 minutes. Meanwhile, quarter 1 of the yellow onions. Place in a small baking pan with the garlic and ginger. Drizzle with the canola oil and toss the onion mixture to coat them with the oil. Place in the oven and roast alongside the beef bones until slightly charred, about 30 minutes. Stir the beef bones once during this time.

Transfer the beef bones and onion mixture to a stockpot. Quarter the parsnips and add to the pot with the star anise, cinnamon stick, salt, and 3 qt (3 l) water. Place over high heat and bring to a boil, stirring occasionally and skimming off any foam from the surface. Reduce the heat to medium and boil gently, uncovered, until the broth takes on a rich brown color, about 1 hour. Line a fine-mesh sieve with cheesecloth (muslin) and place over a clean saucepan. Remove and discard the bones from the stock, then pour the stock through the sieve and discard the solids. Add the fish sauce, 1 tablespoon of the vinegar, and the white pepper. Place over low heat and keep at a low boil.

In a bowl, soak the rice vermicelli in warm water to cover for 15 minutes. Drain and set aside. Slice the beef against the grain into slices ⅛ inch (3 mm) thick (page 22). Cut the remaining 2 yellow onions into thin slices. Thinly slice the green onions on the diagonal. In a bowl, toss together the green and yellow onions, cilantro, chile sauce, and remaining 1 tablespoon vinegar.

Bring a saucepan three-fourths full of water to a boil. Add the drained noodles and boil until just tender, about 2 minutes. Drain. Divide the noodles, beef slices, and onion–chile sauce mixture among bowls. Top with the broth. Pass the garnishes and Nuoc Cham for diners to add as desired to the soup.

MAKES 6–8 SERVINGS

2 lb (1 kg) beef bones with marrow

3 yellow onions

5 cloves garlic

3-inch (7.5-cm) piece fresh ginger

1 tablespoon canola oil

2 parsnips, peeled

5 star anise

1 cinnamon stick

1 teaspoon salt

¼ cup (2 fl oz/60 ml) fish sauce

2 tablespoons rice vinegar

½ teaspoon ground white pepper

1 lb (500 g) rice vermicelli

1 lb (500 g) beef sirloin, 5 inches (13 cm) thick

3 green (spring) onions

2 tablespoons chopped fresh cilantro (fresh coriander)

1 tablespoon Sriracha chile sauce (page 115)

Garnishes *(far left)*

Nuoc Cham (page 111) for serving

SPICY TOFU AND BAMBOO SHOOT SOUP

1 cup (3 oz/90 g) fresh shiitake mushrooms

4-by-4-by-1½-inch (10-by-10-by-4-cm) block firm tofu

5 green (spring) onions

⅓ cup (2 oz/60 g) *each* julienned chicken breast meat and julienned beef sirloin

½ cup (2 oz/60 g) julienned canned bamboo shoots

1 tablespoon canola oil

1 tablespoon peeled and minced fresh ginger

8 cups (64 fl oz/2 l) low-sodium chicken broth

⅓ cup (3 fl oz/80 ml) black vinegar (page 76)

2 tablespoons *each* Chinese rice wine and chile bean paste *(far right)*

1 tablespoon *each* dark soy sauce and Asian sesame oil

¼ teaspoon ground white pepper

3 tablespoons cornstarch (cornflour)

2 large eggs, beaten

¼ cup (1½ oz/45 g) English peas

3 tablespoons julienned smoked ham

Remove the stems from the mushrooms and discard. Cut the caps into fine julienne. Cut the tofu into fine julienne. Thinly slice the green onions, including the tender green parts, on the diagonal. Set aside.

In a large pot over high heat, bring 2 qt (2 l) water to a boil. Add the chicken, beef, bamboo shoots, mushrooms, and tofu and cook for 3 minutes. Drain and set aside.

Rinse the pot, place over high heat, and heat the canola oil. Add 4 of the sliced green onions and the ginger and sauté until fragrant, about 2 minutes. Stir in the tofu mixture along with the broth, vinegar, rice wine, chile bean paste, soy sauce, sesame oil, and white pepper. Bring to a boil and boil for 1 minute. Reduce the heat to low and simmer, uncovered, for 10 minutes to blend the flavors.

In a small bowl, stir together the cornstarch and 6 tablespoons (3 fl oz/90 ml) water. Swirl the eggs into the gently simmering soup; they will form strands of cooked egg. (Do not allow the soup to boil, or the eggs will scramble.) Slowly pour about half of the cornstarch mixture into the soup while stirring constantly. The soup will thicken slightly. Add more of the cornstarch mixture as desired for a thicker consistency.

Ladle the soup into warmed bowls. Garnish with the peas, ham, and remaining sliced green onion, dividing evenly. Serve immediately.

MAKES 4–6 SERVINGS

CHILE BEAN PASTE

Popular in Sichuan and Hunan cooking, chile bean paste is a thick cooking sauce and condiment primarily made from fermented soybeans mixed with chiles, garlic, and vinegar. It adds an intense and fiery flavor to clay-pot dishes, meat marinades, and stir-fries. Look for it in glass jars or cans, sometimes labeled "hot bean paste" or "Sichuan chile sauce." Do not confuse chile bean paste with chile pastes or chile sauces, condiments and seasonings that range from sweet to pungent and are typically made by grinding fresh or dried chiles to a paste with other seasonings.

INDONESIAN SPICY CHICKEN NOODLE SOUP

FRYING SHALLOTS

Shallots, which are covered with a golden brown or purplish skin, grow in a similar way to garlic, with a number of small bulbs clustered together at the root end. Milder than onions, shallots are used throughout Southeast Asia as an aromatic base for dishes, and are thinly sliced and fried for garnishing soups, fried rice, and noodles. To fry shallots, heat 3 tablespoons canola or peanut oil in a small frying pan over medium-high heat. Add 3 thinly sliced shallots (about ½ cup/ 2 oz/60 g), and sauté until crisp and dark brown, 7–10 minutes. Using a slotted spoon, transfer to paper towels to drain.

In a saucepan over high heat, bring 8 cups (64 fl oz/2 l) water to a boil. Add the 1 tablespoon salt and the chicken, and return to a boil. Reduce the heat to medium and cook, uncovered, until the chicken is opaque throughout when tested with a knife, about 30 minutes. Using tongs, transfer the chicken to a plate to cool. Reserve the broth. Meanwhile, soak the vermicelli in water to cover for 15 minutes. Drain and set aside.

Seed and chop 1 of the chiles. Chop 4 of the shallots and the ginger slices. In a mortar, combine the chile, chopped shallots, ginger, garlic, almonds, lemongrass, turmeric, and coriander and grind together until a paste forms. Add 1–2 tablespoons water if needed to facilitate grinding. Set the chile paste aside. Slice the remaining 3 shallots and fry until crisp *(left)*.

In a large saucepan over medium heat, heat the canola oil. Add the chile paste and sauté until fragrant, about 2 minutes. Pour the reserved broth through a fine-mesh sieve into the saucepan and bring to a boil. Reduce the heat to low and simmer, uncovered, for 15 minutes. Stir in the fish sauce and lemon juice, season to taste with salt and pepper, and simmer for 5 minutes.

Shred the chicken into thin pieces, discarding the bones. Halve the remaining chile lengthwise, remove the seeds, and thinly slice on the diagonal. Quarter the hard-boiled eggs lengthwise.

Bring a large saucepan three-fourths full of water to a boil, add the drained noodles, and cook until just tender, about 2 minutes. Drain and divide among warmed individual bowls.

Divide the shredded chicken, bean sprouts, cilantro, green onions, and sliced chile evenly among the bowls. Ladle the hot broth over the top and garnish with the eggs and fried shallots. Serve at once.

MAKES 4–6 SERVINGS

1 tablespoon salt, plus salt to taste

½ lb (250 g) *each* bone-in chicken breasts and bone-in chicken thighs, skin removed

¾ lb (375 g) rice vermicelli

2 green jalapeño chiles

7 shallots

2 fresh ginger slices, peeled

3 cloves garlic, chopped

5 blanched almonds

2 tablespoons chopped lemongrass

½ teaspoon ground turmeric

¼ teaspoon ground coriander

2 tablespoons canola oil

2 tablespoons *each* fish sauce and fresh lemon juice

Ground black pepper

3 hard-boiled eggs (page 113)

1 cup (1 oz/30 g) mung bean sprouts

¼ cup (⅓ oz/10 g) chopped fresh cilantro (fresh coriander)

3 green (spring) onions, sliced on the diagonal

THAI SHRIMP AND LEMONGRASS SOUP

4 cloves garlic

2 green serrano chiles, seeded and chopped

3 tablespoons chopped fresh cilantro (fresh coriander) stems

1½ teaspoons black peppercorns, coarsely ground

8–10 fresh shiitake mushrooms

3 lemongrass stalks

4 fresh galangal slices (page 113), each ¼ inch (6 mm) thick

2 tablespoons canola or peanut oil

4 shallots, thinly sliced

8 cups (64 fl oz/2 l) low-sodium chicken broth

1½ teaspoons finely grated lime zest

¼ cup (2 fl oz/60 ml) *each* fish sauce and fresh lime juice

1 tablespoon chopped palm sugar (page 98) or brown sugar

1 lb (500 g) shrimp (prawns), peeled and deveined (page 115)

¼ cup (⅓ oz/10 g) *each* shredded fresh Thai basil and fresh cilantro (fresh coriander)

In a mortar, combine the garlic, chiles, cilantro stems, and pepper and grind together with a pestle until a thick paste forms, adding 1 tablespoon water if needed to facilitate grinding. Alternatively, combine all the ingredients in a mini food processor and process to a paste. Set the chile paste aside.

Remove and discard the stems from the mushrooms. Thinly slice the caps. Trim and crush the lemongrass stalks *(right)*. Smash the galangal slices with the side of a chef's knife.

In a stockpot over high heat, heat the canola oil. Add the mushrooms and sauté until they begin to brown, about 2 minutes. Stir in the lemongrass, galangal slices, and shallots and sauté until fragrant, about 2 minutes longer.

Pour in the broth, add the lime zest, and bring to a boil. Reduce the heat to medium, stir in the chile paste, and simmer for 3–4 minutes. Add the fish sauce, lime juice, and palm sugar and stir to mix well. Simmer the soup for 5 minutes to allow the flavors to develop.

Just before serving, stir in the shrimp. As soon as they begin to turn color and are opaque, after about 3 minutes, remove the soup from the heat. Ladle the soup into individual bowls, garnish with the shredded herbs, and serve at once.

MAKES 6 SERVINGS

PREPARING LEMONGRASS

Lemongrass, a long, fibrous, grayish green grass with a paler bulblike base and a mild lemon fragrance, is a staple herb of Southeast Asia, where it is used to flavor soups, curry pastes, and other preparations. To use it, peel away any dry leaves from the base and trim off the grassy top section. To maximize the citrus flavor, crush the base and stem with the flat side of chef's knife or cleaver before slicing or using. If using lemongrass in large pieces, remove it before serving the dish.

RICE PLATES

Rice, nutritious and comforting, is Asia's most common starch and is served alongside myriad savory dishes. Here you will find simple directions for cooking a pot of rice, along with recipes in which rice serves as an accompaniment, such as Chinese steamed fish and Thai beef curry. In the Indian biryani *and Malaysian fried rice, it is a main ingredient.*

CARAMELIZED CHICKEN WITH GINGER

In a Dutch oven over high heat, heat the canola oil. Add the chicken and sear on all sides until golden brown, 10–15 minutes. Transfer the chicken to a plate. Drain off most of the fat from the pan. Set the pan aside without rinsing.

To make the caramel sauce, in a deep saucepan over low heat, combine the sugar, lemon juice, and 3 tablespoons water and heat, stirring occasionally, to dissolve the sugar. In a separate saucepan over low heat, combine the fish sauce, soy sauce, and ¼ cup (2 fl oz/60 ml) water and heat until the sauce comes to a simmer; set aside. Raise the heat to high under the saucepan containing the sugar, bring to a boil, and boil, without stirring, until the mixture caramelizes and turns amber, 10–12 minutes. Remove from the heat and carefully pour the warm fish sauce mixture into the sugar mixture. The sugar will bubble vigorously. Stir until a smooth sauce forms, then set aside.

Return the Dutch oven to medium heat. When the fat remaining in the pan is hot, add the shallots, garlic, 1 tablespoon ginger, and pepper and sauté until the shallots begin to wilt, about 2 minutes. Return the chicken pieces to the pan and pour the warm caramel sauce over the top. Reduce the heat to medium-low, cover, and simmer the chicken until nearly tender, about 20 minutes. Uncover the chicken and continue to simmer until the meat is very tender, about 10 minutes longer. Stir the chicken once or twice while it cooks.

Transfer the chicken and sauce to a warmed serving dish. Garnish with the green onions and 1 teaspoon ginger. Serve accompanied with the rice.

Note: Drumettes are the large wing joints—the meatiest section— of chicken or other poultry wings.

MAKES 4 MAIN-COURSE SERVINGS OR 6–8 SMALLER SERVINGS

PREPARING GINGER

A light brown, fibrous, and knobby rhizome with a sweet yet piquant flavor, fresh ginger is julienned, sliced, chopped, or grated for use in soups or salads or in steamed, stir-fried, or braised dishes. Here it is used in a Vietnamese chicken dish, but it turns up in pantries throughout Asia. Look for ginger that is firm and with skin that is light, smooth, and shiny. Use a vegetable peeler or a small, sharp knife to remove the thin skin. To grate ginger, use the finest rasps on a handheld grater or a flat ceramic grater designed for the task.

2 tablespoons canola or peanut oil

2 lb (1 kg) chicken wings or drumettes (see Note)

FOR THE CARAMEL SAUCE:

½ cup (4 oz/125 g) sugar

1 tablespoon fresh lemon juice

¼ cup (2 fl oz/60 ml) fish sauce

1 tablespoon light soy sauce

4 shallots, thinly sliced

2 cloves garlic, minced

1 tablespoon peeled and finely julienned fresh ginger, plus 1 teaspoon peeled and very finely julienned fresh ginger

½ teaspoon ground black pepper

2 green (spring) onions, thinly sliced on the diagonal

3 cups (15 oz/470 g) cooked long-grain white rice (page 61)

LAMB BIRYANI

1 lb (500 g) lamb
tenderloin

3 tablespoons clarified
butter (page 112)

2 yellow onions, thinly
sliced, plus ½ cup (2 oz/
60 g) chopped yellow
onion

5 cloves garlic, chopped

2 tablespoons peeled and
chopped fresh ginger

1 green jalapeño chile,
seeded and chopped

Spice mixture (far right)

½ cup (4 oz/125 g) plain
yogurt

2 tablespoons fresh
lemon juice

2 teaspoons salt

1½ cups (10½ oz/330 g)
basmati rice

¼ cup (⅓ oz/10 g)
chopped fresh cilantro
(fresh coriander)

¼ cup (1½ oz/45 g)
unsalted raw cashews,
toasted (page 102) and
chopped

¼ cup (1½ oz/45 g) golden
raisins (sultanas)

2 hard-boiled eggs
(page 113), peeled and
cut into wedges

Cut the lamb into ½-inch (12-mm) cubes. In a Dutch oven over
high heat, heat 1 tablespoon of the clarified butter. Working in
batches, sear the lamb cubes in a single layer until deep brown on
all sides, 7–10 minutes per batch. Transfer to a plate.

Return the Dutch oven to medium heat and heat 1 tablespoon of
the clarified butter. Add the 2 sliced onions and sauté until crisp
and brown, 15–20 minutes. Using a slotted spoon, transfer the
onions to paper towels to drain. While the onions are cooking, in
a blender, combine the ½ cup chopped onion, garlic, ginger, and
chile and process until a thick paste forms. Add 1–2 tablespoons
water if needed to facilitate blending.

Preheat the oven to 350°F (180°C).

Return the Dutch oven to medium-high heat and heat the
remaining 1 tablespoon clarified butter. Add the onion-garlic
paste and sauté until golden brown, 5–7 minutes. Add the spice
mixture and sauté until fragrant, about 2 minutes. Add the
browned onions, the yogurt, the lemon juice, 1½ teaspoons of
the salt, and ¼ cup (2 fl oz/60 ml) water. Reduce the heat to low
and simmer for 2 minutes to blend the flavors. Stir in the seared
lamb, mix well, cover, and simmer for 10 minutes to heat through.

Raise the heat to medium, stir the rice into the lamb, and sauté
briefly. Add 2 cups (16 fl oz/500 ml) water and the remaining
½ teaspoon salt and bring to a simmer. Stir well, cover, and place
in the oven. Bake until the rice is cooked through and most of the
moisture has evaporated, about 30 minutes; stir once during this
time. Let rest, covered, for 10 minutes. Uncover, fluff the rice and
lamb with a fork, and transfer to a platter. Garnish with the
cilantro, cashews, raisins, and eggs. Serve at once.

MAKES 6–8 SERVINGS

SPICE MIXTURE

Biryani, elaborate dishes of rice
and meat or vegetables, were
introduced to northern India by
the Moghuls in the sixteenth
century. The spice mixtures, or
masalas, used in biryani impart
a rich color and flavor to the
dishes. To make the mixture
called for here, toast and grind
1 teaspoon each cumin and
coriander seeds (page 21).
Transfer the ground seeds to
a bowl and stir in 1 teaspoon
each ground turmeric and
cinnamon, ½ teaspoon ground
cardamom, ¼ teaspoon each
ground nutmeg and cayenne
pepper, 4 whole star anise, and
3 bay leaves.

STEAMED FISH WITH GREEN ONIONS AND GINGER

WOK STEAMING
A wok can easily be converted into a steamer. Place the wok on the stove top and pour in water to a depth of 2–3 inches (5–7.5 cm). Set a bamboo steamer (or a cake cooling rack) in the wok, making sure that it sits above the water. Bring the water to a boil and place the plate holding the food on the steamer. To ensure that the steam circulates freely, the plate should be about 2 inches (5 cm) smaller in diameter than the wok. Cover with a tight lid and steam the dish until done.

Measure the fish fillets at their thickest point. Make a bed of the halved green onions on a plate large enough to hold the fish and suitable for steaming *(left)*. Place the fillets in a single layer on the bed of green onions. Cover and refrigerate until ready to steam.

Place a bamboo steamer on the bottom of a wok or large, deep frying pan and pour in water to a depth of 2 inches (5 cm). The water should not touch the steamer. Bring the water to a boil over high heat.

Meanwhile, in a bowl, stir together the ginger, garlic, 1 tablespoon of the canola oil, light soy sauce, sesame oil, dark soy sauce, oyster sauce, sugar, cornstarch, and white pepper. Spoon the mixture evenly over the fish fillets.

Place the plate on the steamer above the boiling water, cover tightly, and steam the fish over high heat for 10 minutes per inch (2.5 cm) thickness. Carefully remove the plate from the steamer and transfer the fish fillets to a warmed platter. Discard the bed of green onions and spoon any sauce remaining on the plate over the fish.

In a small pan over high heat, heat the remaining 1 tablespoon canola oil until it is almost smoking. Place the julienned green onion on top of the fish. Carefully drizzle the hot oil over the fish and serve with the rice.

MAKES 4–6 SERVINGS

4 sea bass or halibut fillets, 6 oz (185 g) each

3 green (spring) onions, halved crosswise, plus 1 green onion, finely julienned

1 tablespoon peeled and finely julienned fresh ginger

2 cloves garlic, minced

2 tablespoons canola or peanut oil

1 tablespoon light soy sauce

2 teaspoons Asian sesame oil

1½ teaspoons dark soy sauce

1½ teaspoons oyster sauce

1 teaspoon sugar

1 teaspoon cornstarch (cornflour)

⅛ teaspoon ground white pepper

3 cups (15 oz/470 g) cooked long-grain white rice (page 61)

MALAYSIAN SPICY FRIED RICE WITH SHRIMP

3 *each* shallots and cloves garlic, chopped

2 fresh hot red chiles, seeded and chopped

1 tablespoon peeled and chopped fresh galangal (page 113)

1 teaspoon shrimp paste (page 114)

2 tablespoons *each* fish sauce and sweet soy sauce

1½ tablespoons fresh lime juice

1 teaspoon Sriracha chile sauce (page 115)

3 cups (15 oz/470 g) cooked long-grain white rice, cold *(far right)*

1 cup (5 oz/155 g) diced carrots

4 tablespoons (2 fl oz/60 ml) canola or peanut oil

2 cups (6 oz/185 g) diced napa cabbage

½ lb (250 g) shrimp (prawns), peeled and deveined (page 115), then cut into ¼-inch (6-mm) dice

3 eggs, beaten

¼ cup (1½ oz/45 g) fresh or frozen English peas

3 shallots, thinly sliced and fried crisp (page 48)

In a mortar, combine the shallots, garlic, chiles, galangal, and shrimp paste and grind together with a pestle, gradually adding 3 tablespoons water as you work to form a paste. Alternatively, combine the ingredients in a mini food processor and process to a paste. Set the chile paste aside.

In a small bowl, stir together the fish sauce, sweet soy sauce, lime juice, and chile sauce. Set the sauce mixture aside.

Place the cooked rice in a wide bowl and gently press out any lumps to separate the grains. Bring a small saucepan three-fourths full of water to a boil. Add the carrots and cook for 5 minutes. Drain and rinse under running cold water.

In a large wok or sauté pan over high heat, heat 3 tablespoons of the canola oil until almost smoking. Add the chile paste and fry until fragrant, about 1 minute. Stir in the cabbage and carrots and stir-fry until the cabbage begins to wilt, about 5 minutes. Add the shrimp and continue to stir-fry until they just turn opaque, about 3 minutes. Transfer to a bowl.

Return the pan to high heat and add the remaining 1 tablespoon oil. When it is hot, add the eggs and scramble until just set, about 2 minutes. Add the rice and peas and return the cabbage mixture to the pan. Stir-fry until the rice is heated through, 5–7 minutes. Pour in the sauce mixture and continue to sauté until the rice is well seasoned, about 3 minutes longer. Transfer the rice mixture to a warmed bowl, garnish with the fried shallots, and serve.

MAKES 4–6 SERVINGS

COOKING RICE

Of the various methods for cooking rice, the absorption method is arguably the most foolproof. Place 1 cup (7 oz/ 220 g) long-grain white rice in a fine-mesh sieve and rinse until the water runs clear. Transfer the rice to a heavy saucepan and add 1½ cups (12 fl oz/375 ml) water. Bring to a boil and give the rice a quick stir. Reduce the heat to low, cover, and cook for 20 minutes. Do not stir or remove the lid. Remove from the heat and let rest, covered, for 10 minutes. Fluff the rice with a fork before serving. Makes about 3 cups (15 oz/470 g) cooked rice.

THAI RED CURRY BEEF

In a large sauté pan over high heat, heat the canola oil until it is almost smoking. Add the onion and the red and green bell peppers and stir-fry just until tender, 5–7 minutes. Transfer the vegetables to a bowl.

Return the pan to medium heat and add the coconut milk. Heat until it begins to bubble. Stir in the curry paste and simmer until the sauce begins to bubble, 3–5 minutes. Stir in the fish sauce, palm sugar, tamarind concentrate, and lime juice and bring to a low boil. Cook until the sauce begins to thicken, 7–10 minutes. Stir in the beef and vegetables and continue to simmer until the meat is just cooked through, 5–7 minutes.

Transfer the curry to a warmed serving bowl. Garnish with the peanuts and basil and serve at once with the rice.

MAKES 4–6 SERVINGS

THAI RED CURRY PASTE

To make the red curry paste used in this dish, in a mortar, combine 2 red jalapeño chiles, seeded and chopped; 3 cloves garlic, chopped; 2 shallots, chopped; 1 tablespoon peeled and chopped fresh galangal (page 113); 1 lemongrass stalk, bulb only, chopped; 1 table-spoon chopped fresh cilantro (fresh coriander) stems; 1 tablespoon ground coriander; 2 teaspoons ground cumin; and ½ teaspoon shrimp paste (page 114). Grind together with a pestle until a paste forms, adding 1–2 tablespoons water if needed to facilitate blending.

1 tablespoon canola or peanut oil

1 yellow onion, thinly sliced

1 *each* red and green bell peppers (capsicums), seeded and sliced lengthwise into ¼-inch (6-mm) strips

1 cup (8 fl oz/250 ml) coconut milk

Thai Red Curry Paste *(far left)*

¼ cup (2 fl oz/60 ml) fish sauce

2 tablespoons chopped palm sugar (page 98)

1½ teaspoons tamarind concentrate (page 115)

1 teaspoon fresh lime juice

1 lb (500 g) beef tenderloin, cut across the grain into slices ¼ inch (6 mm) thick

2 tablespoons unsalted peanuts, toasted (page 102) and chopped

5 fresh Thai basil sprigs

3 cups (15 oz/470 g) cooked long-grain white rice (page 61)

STIR-FRIED PORK IN BLACK BEAN SAUCE

¾ lb (375 g) pork tenderloin

½ teaspoon baking soda
(bicarbonate of soda)

¼ teaspoon *each* salt
and sugar

⅛ teaspoon ground
white pepper

FOR THE SAUCE:

1½ tablespoons fermented
black beans, well rinsed

1 tablespoon *each* oyster
sauce and light soy sauce

1 teaspoon *each* Asian
sesame oil, sugar, and
cornstarch (cornflour)

⅛ teaspoon ground
white pepper

1 small yellow onion

½ *each* small green and red
bell peppers (capsicums)

2 tablespoons canola oil

2 cloves garlic

2 fresh ginger slices

1 tablespoon Chinese
rice wine

Fresh cilantro (fresh
coriander) sprigs

3 cups (15 oz/470 g)
cooked long-grain white
rice (page 61)

Cut the pork into 1-inch (2.5-cm) cubes. In a bowl, combine the pork, baking soda, salt, sugar, white pepper, and 2 tablespoons water and mix well. Cover and marinate in the refrigerator for at least 1 hour or for up to 3 hours.

To make the sauce, in a bowl, stir together the black beans, oyster sauce, soy sauce, sesame oil, sugar, cornstarch, white pepper, and ¼ cup (2 fl oz/60 ml) water. Set aside.

Dice the onion. Cut the bell pepper halves into cubes. Set aside. In a wok or large sauté pan over high heat, heat 1 tablespoon of the canola oil until almost smoking. Add the garlic and ginger and fry until golden brown, about 4–5 seconds. Using a slotted spoon, lift out the garlic and ginger and discard. Add the onion and bell peppers and stir-fry until just tender, about 5 minutes. Add the rice wine and deglaze the pan, stirring to scrape up any brown bits from the bottom. When the wine has nearly evaporated, transfer the vegetables to a bowl.

Remove the pork cubes from the marinade and pat dry with paper towels. Discard the marinade. Return the pan to high heat and heat until very hot. Add the remaining 1 tablespoon oil to the hot pan. When it is hot, add the pork and stir-fry until it browns and turns opaque, about 3 minutes. Transfer the meat to a colander to drain.

Return the pan to high heat and heat until very hot. Add the cooked vegetables, the pork, and the sauce and stir-fry rapidly until the sauce thickens and the mixture is heated through, about 5 minutes.

Transfer the pork mixture to a warmed platter, garnish with cilantro sprigs, and serve with the rice.

MAKES 4–6 SERVINGS

FERMENTED BLACK BEANS
Sometimes called salted or preserved black beans, fermented black beans are soybeans that have been dried, salted, and allowed to ferment until they turn black. They are distinctly pungent, have an almost smoky character, and are used mainly in Chinese cooking, such as in this simple pork stir-fry. Before using the beans, gently rinse them in a fine-mesh sieve to remove excess salt and then prepare according to the recipe. Sold in plastic bags, fermented black beans will keep for a year in a cool, dry place.

NOODLE DISHES

Asian pantries hold a profusion of noodles made from wheat, rice, and beans in countless sizes, shapes, and textures. This remarkable variety invites the creation of a nearly limitless selection of hot and cold specialties, from chilled Japanese buckwheat noodles to steaming-hot stir-fried egg noodles, served as filling one-dish meals or as part of a menu.

VIETNAMESE GRILLED CHICKEN
WITH RICE NOODLES
68

COLD SOBA WITH DIPPING SAUCE
71

CELLOPHANE NOODLE SALAD
72

MALAYSIAN STIR-FRIED NOODLES WITH BEEF
75

PAN-SEARED FISH WITH NOODLES
76

VIETNAMESE GRILLED CHICKEN WITH RICE NOODLES

Place the chicken pieces in a large, shallow bowl. In a mortar, combine the garlic, shallots, cilantro stems, galangal, salt, and pepper and grind together with a pestle to form a paste, adding 1 tablespoon water if needed to facilitate grinding. Transfer the paste to a bowl and stir in the coconut milk, fish sauce, rice wine, soy sauce, and peanut oil. Pour the marinade over the chicken pieces, then turn the chicken and coat evenly. Cover and refrigerate for at least 2 hours or for up to overnight.

Prepare a hot fire in a charcoal grill, or preheat the oven to 450°F (230°C). Remove the chicken from the marinade and shake off the excess. Discard the marinade. Place the chicken pieces on the grill rack directly over the coals and grill, turning until browned on both sides, 5–7 minutes. Using tongs, move the chicken to the side of the rack away from the direct heat. Cover and continue to cook the chicken, turning once, until the juices run clear when a thigh is pierced, 15–20 minutes. If cooking in the oven, place the chicken pieces on a rack in a roasting pan and roast until the juices run clear when a thigh is pierced, 35–40 minutes. An instant-read thermometer inserted into the thickest part of the thigh away from the bone should register 170°F (77°C).

Just before the chicken is ready, bring a saucepan three-fourths full of water to a boil. Add the rice vermicelli and cook until just tender, about 1 minute. Drain, place in a bowl, and toss with ¼ cup (2 fl oz/60 ml) of the Nuoc Cham.

Spread the noodles on a warmed platter and arrange the chicken pieces on top. Garnish with the chile, carrots, and cilantro sprigs. Serve with the remaining Nuoc Cham for dipping.

MAKES 6–8 SERVINGS

1 chicken, 3 lb (1.5 kg), quartered

4 cloves garlic, chopped

2 shallots, chopped

1 tablespoon *each* chopped fresh cilantro (fresh coriander) stems and peeled and minced fresh galangal (page 113)

1 teaspoon salt

¼ teaspoon ground black pepper

⅓ cup (3 fl oz/80 ml) coconut milk

2 tablespoons *each* fish sauce and Chinese rice wine

1 tablespoon *each* dark soy sauce and peanut oil

½ lb (250 g) rice vermicelli, soaked in warm water for 15 minutes

Nuoc Cham (page 111) for serving

1 fresh hot red chile, seeded and thinly sliced

¼ cup (1 oz/30 g) very finely julienned carrots

4 or 5 fresh cilantro (fresh coriander) sprigs

MALAYSIAN STIR-FRIED NOODLES WITH BEEF

¾ lb (375 g) fresh or dried flat rice stick noodles

½ lb (250 g) beef tenderloin

1 teaspoon cornstarch (cornflour)

¼ teaspoon *each* salt and sugar

⅛ teaspoon baking soda (bicarbonate of soda)

3 tablespoons low-sodium beef broth or chicken broth

1 tablespoon *each* fish sauce, dark soy sauce, and sweet soy sauce

1 teaspoon rice vinegar

½ teaspoon Sriracha chile sauce (page 115)

3 tablespoons canola oil

2 cloves garlic, minced

1 tablespoon peeled and minced fresh ginger

1 yellow onion, thinly sliced

1 cup (4 oz/125 g) julienned red bell pepper (capsicum)

½ cup (½ oz/15 g) mung bean sprouts

¼ cup (⅓ oz/10 g) sliced garlic chives *(far right)*

If using dried rice stick noodles, soak them in warm water to cover for 30 minutes and then drain. Slice the beef across the grain into strips 4 inches (10 cm) long by ¼ inch (6 mm) wide. In a bowl, combine the cornstarch, salt, sugar, baking soda, 1 tablespoon water, and beef strips and stir to mix. Cover and marinate in the refrigerator for 30 minutes.

In another bowl, stir together the broth, fish sauce, dark soy sauce, sweet soy sauce, rice vinegar, and chile sauce. Set aside.

In a wok or large sauté pan over high heat, heat 2 tablespoons of the canola oil until very hot. Add the garlic and ginger and stir-fry until fragrant, 4–5 seconds. Add the onion and bell pepper and stir-fry until just tender, 3–4 minutes. Transfer the vegetables to a bowl.

Return the pan to high heat, add the remaining 1 tablespoon oil, and heat until very hot. Remove the beef from the marinade and pat dry with paper towels. Discard the marinade. Add the beef to the pan and stir-fry until it just turns opaque, about 2 minutes. Transfer the beef to a colander and let drain.

Return the pan to high heat and add the fish sauce mixture. Bring to a boil and add the fresh or reconstituted noodles and the stir-fried vegetables. Cover and simmer until most of the sauce has been absorbed by the noodles, about 2 minutes for fresh noodles and 4 minutes for dried. Uncover, return the beef to the pan, and add the bean sprouts and garlic chives. Stir-fry until the meat is heated through, about 2 minutes. Transfer to a warmed serving platter and serve at once.

MAKES 4–6 SERVINGS

CHINESE CHIVES

The term *Chinese chives* is applied to a trio of distinct chives used in Chinese and Southeast Asian cooking. Flowering chives have dark green, firm stalks, small, pointed flower buds, and a relatively sharp flavor. Yellow chives have long, pale yellow blades (they are blanched, that is, deprived of the sun as they mature) and a sweet, subtle flavor. When grown in the sun, these same chives have emerald green blades and a pleasant garlic-onion flavor, which accounts for their other name, garlic chives.

PAN-SEARED FISH WITH NOODLES

Preheat the oven to 400°F (200°C).

To make the noodles, bring a large saucepan three-fourths full of water to a boil. Separate the noodles with your fingers, add them to the boiling water, and boil just until tender, 2–3 minutes. Drain and rinse under running cold water, then drain again. In a large bowl, toss the noodles with the sesame oil, salt, green onions, and sesame seeds. Use your fingers to distribute the seasoning evenly and separate the strands.

In a 10-inch (25-cm) nonstick frying pan over medium-high heat, heat 2–3 tablespoons of the canola oil. Arrange the noodles in a coil in the pan and press down on them with a small plate. Cook until golden brown on the bottom, 7–10 minutes, adjusting the heat so that the noodles sizzle but do not scorch. Turn the noodles and drizzle 2 tablespoons canola oil under the noodles. Cook until the second side is golden brown, 7–10 minutes. Transfer the noodles to a baking sheet lined with paper towels to drain.

Meanwhile, cook the fish. Season the fillets with the salt and white pepper. In a large sauté pan over high heat, warm 1 tablespoon of the canola oil. Add the fillets in a single layer and cook, turning once, until golden brown on both sides, 2–3 minutes per side. Transfer the fish to a baking sheet and place in the oven for 5 minutes for fillets 1 inch (2.5 cm) thick and 10 minutes for fillets 2 inches (5 cm) thick. Set the sauté pan aside without rinsing.

(Continued on next page.)

BLACK VINEGAR

Chinese black vinegars are made by fermenting a grain (rice, wheat, millet, sorghum) and leaving it to age. They are generally a deep reddish black and have a rich, smoky, pleasantly tart taste. Eastern China produces good black vinegars made from glutinous rice, with their complex flavors a result of slow aging. Look for bottles labeled "Chinkiang vinegar" for the finest examples. Black vinegar is used to flavor soups, stir-fried noodles, and braises; to serve as a dipping sauce for dumplings; and to make sweet-and-sour dishes.

FOR THE NOODLES:

½ lb (250 g) fresh Chinese egg noodles

1 tablespoon Asian sesame oil

¾ teaspoon salt

¼ cup (1¼ oz/37 g) diagonally sliced green (spring) onions

½ teaspoon sesame seeds, toasted (page 21)

4–5 tablespoons (2–2½ fl oz/60–75 ml) canola or peanut oil

FOR THE FISH:

4 sea bass or salmon fillets, 6 oz (185 g) each

½ teaspoon salt

¼ teaspoon ground white pepper

3 tablespoons canola or peanut oil

⅓ cup (3 fl oz/80 ml) low-sodium chicken broth

1 tablespoon *each* dark soy sauce and black vinegar *(far left)*

1 teaspoon *each* Chinese rice wine and Asian sesame oil

½ teaspoon Sriracha chile sauce (page 115)

1 teaspoon sugar

½ teaspoon cornstarch (cornflour)

2 green (spring) onions, minced

1 tablespoon *each* minced peeled fresh ginger and minced seeded green jalapeño chile

2 cloves garlic, minced

1 cup (2 oz/60 g) stemmed and julienned fresh shiitake mushrooms

¼ cup (1 oz/30 g) julienned canned bamboo shoots

FOR THE GARNISH:

2 green (spring) onions, thinly sliced on the diagonal

1 red jalapeño chile, seeded and julienned

In a small bowl, stir together the broth, soy sauce, vinegar, rice wine, sesame oil, chile sauce, sugar, and cornstarch, to make a sauce.

Return the sauté pan used for the fish to high heat and add the remaining 2 tablespoons oil. When the oil is hot, add the green onions, ginger, minced chile, and garlic and sauté until fragrant, about 2 minutes. Add the mushrooms and bamboo shoots and continue to sauté until the mushrooms begin to wilt, about 2 minutes. Stir in the sauce, bring the mixture to a low boil, and then quickly reduce the heat. Simmer until the sauce thickens, 2–3 minutes. Remove from the heat.

Place the noodles on a cutting board and cut into quarters. Transfer the noodles to a platter and top with the fish fillets. Spoon the sauce over the fillets. Garnish with the sliced green onions and julienned chile and serve.

MAKES 4 SERVINGS

(Photograph appears on following page.)

BAMBOO SHOOTS

Bamboo shoots, shaped like pointed cones and covered with overlapping pale green and yellow papery leaves, are harvested in the spring and winter, with some winter varieties particularly prized for their mild, sweet flavor and pleasantly crunchy texture. Outside of Asia, the shoots are usually available only in cans or jars, or in bulk immersed in large plastic tubs of water. Before using in a recipe, the shoots should be cooked for a couple of minutes in boiling water to rid them of excess salt.

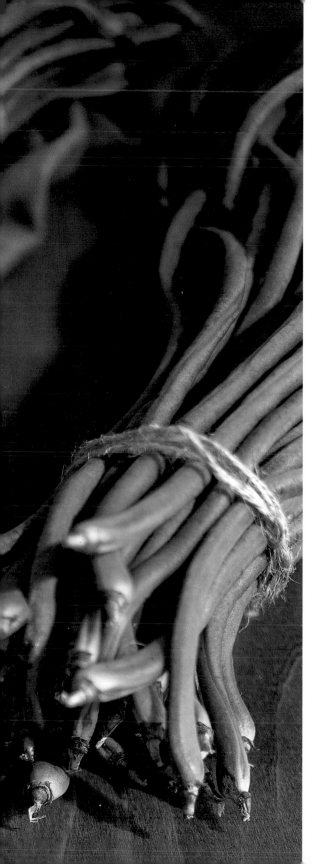

VEGETABLE DISHES

Vegetables are essential elements of the Asian table, and Asian cooks always insist that the produce they buy be both perfectly fresh and in season. Among the colorful dishes created from this bounty are a simple salad of marinated cucumber, a platter of crisp stir-fried long beans or tender sugar snap peas, and eggplant cooked in a flavorful sauce.

THAI MARINATED CUCUMBER SALAD
82

SICHUAN-STYLE BRAISED EGGPLANT
85

SPICY DRY-COOKED LONG BEANS
86

GREEN PAPAYA SALAD
89

STIR-FRIED SUGAR SNAP PEAS
WITH CHINESE SAUSAGE
90

THAI MARINATED CUCUMBER SALAD

Peel the cucumbers, halve lengthwise, and scoop out the seeds (page 113). Cut crosswise into half-moons ¼ inch (6 mm) thick. Place in a colander, sprinkle with 1 teaspoon of the salt, and toss together. Set aside to drain for 1 hour. Pat the cucumbers dry.

In a small saucepan over medium heat, combine the sugar, the remaining 1 teaspoon salt, and the vinegar. Heat until the sugar and salt dissolve, about 2 minutes. Remove from the heat and set aside to cool.

To assemble the salad, in a large bowl, stir together the salted cucumbers, shallots, and chile. Pour the vinegar mixture over the cucumbers and toss well. Garnish with the cilantro leaves. Marinate the cucumbers for at least 1 hour before serving.

MAKES 4–6 SERVINGS

2 lb (1 kg) cucumbers

2 teaspoons salt

2 tablespoons sugar

½ cup (4 fl oz/125 ml) rice vinegar

4 shallots, thinly sliced

1 red jalapeño chile or other fresh hot red chile, seeded and julienned

2 tablespoons fresh cilantro (fresh coriander) leaves

HANDLING FRESH CHILES

Whether you are working with jalapeños, serranos, or any other chiles, always handle them carefully to avoid contact with capsaicin, the compound that gives them their heat. Use a small, sharp knife to trim off the stem and cut the flesh from around the center membrane and seeds, where the capsaicin is concentrated. Discard the stem and core and then mince, chop, slice, or julienne the chile as directed in the recipe. As soon as you have finished, wash your hands, the cutting board, and the knife with soapy hot water.

SICHUAN-STYLE BRAISED EGGPLANT

1½ lb (750 g) Asian (slender) eggplants (aubergines)

1 tablespoon salt

3 tablespoons canola or peanut oil, or as needed

FOR THE SAUCE:

¾ cup (6 fl oz/180 ml) low-sodium chicken broth

1 tablespoon *each* chile bean paste (page 47), black vinegar (page 76), and dark soy sauce

1½ teaspoons light soy sauce

1 teaspoon *each* tomato paste and Asian sesame oil

½ teaspoon *each* sugar and cornstarch (cornflour)

2 cloves garlic, minced

1 tablespoon peeled and minced fresh ginger

¼ cup (1½ oz/45 g) minced celery

1 teaspoon grated or prepared horseradish

¼ lb (125 g) ground (minced) pork

2 green (spring) onions, thinly sliced on the diagonal

Working with 1 eggplant at a time, cut on the diagonal into 1-inch (2.5-cm) pieces. Place the eggplant pieces in a large bowl. Add cold water to cover and stir in the salt. Weight the eggplant pieces with a plate to keep them submerged. Soak for 30 minutes, drain, and pat dry with paper towels.

In a wok or large sauté pan over high heat, heat 2 tablespoons of the canola oil until very hot. Working in 2 batches, add enough eggplant to cover the bottom of the pan in a single layer and stir-fry until crisp and brown on all sides, 7–10 minutes. Using a slotted spoon, transfer to a bowl. Repeat with the remaining eggplant, adding more oil if needed. Set the pan aside without rinsing.

To make the sauce, in a bowl, stir together the broth, chile bean paste, vinegar, dark soy sauce, light soy sauce, tomato paste, sesame oil, sugar, and cornstarch. Set aside.

Return the pan to high heat, add the remaining 1 tablespoon oil, stir in the garlic, ginger, celery, and horseradish, and sauté until just golden brown, about 2 minutes. Stir in the pork and stir-fry until the meat just turns opaque, about 5 minutes.

Add the sauce and bring to a boil. Stir in the eggplant, reduce the heat to low, cover, and braise the eggplant until just tender, 7–10 minutes. Uncover and simmer for a few more minutes until the sauce thickens.

Transfer the eggplant to a warmed bowl and garnish with the green onions. Serve at once.

MAKES 4–6 SERVINGS

ASIAN EGGPLANTS

Native to Southeast Asia, eggplants come in myriad shapes, sizes, and colors, from oblong to round, big to marble-sized, white to nearly black. The two most common Asian eggplant varieties found in the West are the long, slender Chinese and Japanese types. The former have lavender skin, while the latter are usually a deep purple. Both are mild and tender, and contain few seeds. Use either type in this recipe, being sure to slice the eggplant cross-wise on an extreme diagonal to expose as much flesh as possible, thus ensuring quicker, more even cooking.

SPICY DRY-COOKED LONG BEANS

Cut the beans into lengths measuring 3–6 inches (7.5–15 cm). In a wok or large sauté pan over high heat, heat 1 tablespoon of the canola oil until very hot. Add the beans and stir-fry until they begin to char and blister, 7–10 minutes. Transfer the beans to a bowl. Set the pan aside without rinsing.

To make the sauce, in a bowl, stir together the broth, vinegar, soy sauce, tomato paste, chile sauce, cornstarch, and sugar.

Return the pan to high heat, add the remaining 1 tablespoon oil, and heat until very hot. Add the garlic, celery, green onions, and ginger and stir-fry until very fragrant, about 2 minutes. Stir in the pork, chile, and preserved vegetable and continue to stir-fry until the pork is opaque, 2–3 minutes.

Return the beans to the pan and stir-fry for 2 minutes to heat through. Pour the sauce over the beans and stir-fry until the sauce reduces and thickens, 3–4 minutes.

Transfer to a warmed bowl and serve at once.

Note: The term Sichuan preserved vegetable *refers to radishes, mustard greens, napa cabbage, or turnips that have been pickled in vinegar, salt, chile paste, and Sichuan peppercorns. The pickled vegetables have a salty taste and crunchy texture. They are sold wrapped in plastic or in cans or earthenware jugs. Rinse before use to remove excess brine.*

MAKES 4–6 SERVINGS

LONG BEANS

Grown in China and in much of Southeast Asia, these long, slender, pencil-thin beans, also known as yard-long beans and snake beans, are available in two basic types: a somewhat fibrous, pale green variety and a denser, crunchier dark green one. When cooked, they have a mild flavor and a dry, crunchy bite unlike that of other green beans, for they are members of a different genus. The subtle flavor of long beans blends well with spicy and pungent seasonings, as in this Sichuan recipe. Look for beans that are flexible, but not completely limp, and free of dark spots.

1 lb (500 g) long beans or green beans, trimmed

2 tablespoons canola or peanut oil

FOR THE SAUCE:

2 tablespoons low-sodium chicken broth

1 tablespoon *each* black vinegar (page 76) and dark soy sauce

½ teaspoon *each* tomato paste and Sriracha chile sauce (page 115)

½ teaspoon cornstarch (cornflour)

¼ teaspoon sugar

2 cloves garlic, minced

3 tablespoons minced celery

2 tablespoons minced green (spring) onions

1 tablespoon peeled and minced fresh ginger

¼ lb (125 g) ground (minced) pork

1 tablespoon seeded and minced fresh hot red chile

2 tablespoons rinsed and minced Sichuan preserved vegetable (see Note)

GREEN PAPAYA SALAD

1½ lb (750 g) green papayas (about 2), peeled, seeded, and shredded *(far right)*

1 carrot, peeled and shredded

4 shallots, thinly sliced

1 fresh hot red chile, seeded and sliced into thin rings

FOR THE DRESSING:

2 cloves garlic, chopped

1 shallot, chopped

1 teaspoon sugar

¼ teaspoon salt

¼ cup (2 fl oz/60 ml) rice vinegar

3 tablespoons fish sauce

2 tablespoons fresh lime juice

2 teaspoons Sriracha chile sauce (page 115)

3 tablespoons canola or peanut oil

2 tablespoons chopped fresh cilantro (fresh coriander) leaves

In a large bowl, combine the papayas, carrot, shallots, and chile and toss to mix.

To make the dressing, in a mortar, combine the garlic, shallot, sugar, and salt and grind together with a pestle until a paste forms. Alternatively, combine the ingredients in a mini food processor and process to a paste. Add 1–2 tablespoons water to facilitate grinding if necessary. Transfer the paste to a bowl and whisk in the vinegar, fish sauce, lime juice, and chile sauce. Gradually drizzle in the canola oil while continuing to whisk.

Pour the dressing over the papaya mixture, add the cilantro, toss well, and marinate for 1 hour before serving.

Variation Tip: Unripe mangoes may be used in place of the green papayas. Shred them as directed at right.

Serving Tip: This salad is a good accompaniment to grilled meats and rice.

MAKES 4–6 SERVINGS

SHREDDING GREEN PAPAYA

Thai cooks use green papaya as a raw "vegetable" in salads or pickle it and serve it with rice and grilled meats. When cut open, the hard, immature fruit reveals pale green flesh and white seeds. To shred the papaya, use a vegetable peeler to remove the outer skin, then cut the fruit in half lengthwise and scoop out and discard the seeds. Using the largest holes of a grater-shredder or a mandoline, and holding each papaya half lengthwise, shred the flesh into long, thin julienne. Or, use the shredding blade of a food processor.

STIR-FRIED SUGAR SNAP PEAS
WITH CHINESE SAUSAGE

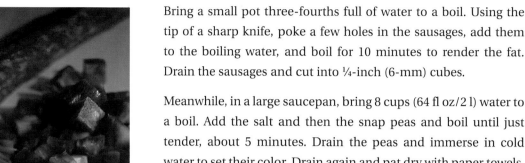

Bring a small pot three-fourths full of water to a boil. Using the tip of a sharp knife, poke a few holes in the sausages, add them to the boiling water, and boil for 10 minutes to render the fat. Drain the sausages and cut into ¼-inch (6-mm) cubes.

Meanwhile, in a large saucepan, bring 8 cups (64 fl oz/2 l) water to a boil. Add the salt and then the snap peas and boil until just tender, about 5 minutes. Drain the peas and immerse in cold water to set their color. Drain again and pat dry with paper towels.

To make the sauce, in a small bowl, stir together the broth, rice wine, sesame oil, cornstarch, salt, sugar, and white pepper. Set the sauce aside.

In a wok or large sauté pan over high heat, heat the canola oil until very hot. Add the ginger and garlic and stir-fry until crisp and brown, about 1 minute. Using a slotted spoon, lift out the ginger and garlic and discard. Add the cubed sausages to the hot pan and stir-fry until just crisp, about 2 minutes. Using the slotted spoon, transfer to paper towels to drain. Reserve the oil in the pan.

Return the pan to high heat, add the snap peas, and stir-fry until they begin to blister, 2–3 minutes. Return the cooked sausages to the pan and stir in the sauce. Continue to stir-fry for several minutes until the sauce thickens.

Transfer to a warmed bowl and serve at once.

MAKES 4–6 SERVINGS

CHINESE SAUSAGE

Known as *lap cheong* in Cantonese, Chinese sausages are air-dried, savory-sweet links made from cured pork, pork fat, salt, sugar, spices, and rice wine. They range from deep red to brown and are similar to dry salami in texture and appearance, although they are generally coarser and always more slender. Darker sausages usually contain duck or pork liver. There is no ideal substitute for *lap cheong*, but a sweet Polish sausage can be used in its place.

¼ lb (125 g) Chinese sausages *(far left)* or sweet Polish sausages

1 tablespoon salt

1½ lb (750 g) sugar snap peas or snow peas (mangetouts), trimmed and strings removed

FOR THE SAUCE:

¼ cup (2 fl oz/60 ml) low-sodium chicken broth

1 tablespoon Chinese rice wine

1 teaspoon Asian sesame oil

1 teaspoon cornstarch (cornflour)

½ teaspoon salt

½ teaspoon sugar

⅛ teaspoon ground white pepper

1 tablespoon canola or peanut oil

3 fresh ginger slices, smashed with the side of a knife

2 cloves garlic

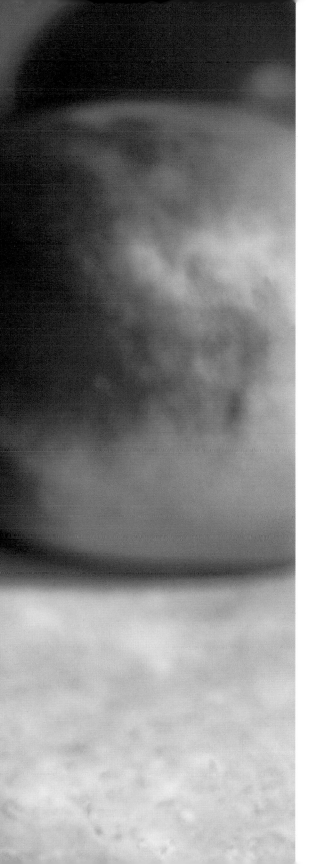

SWEET DISHES

The perfect ending to an Asian meal satisfies the appetite and cleanses the palate. The desserts are traditionally light, ever so slightly sweet, and usually based on fruit. Favorite sweet dishes such as sugar-dusted stuffed banana fritters and a creamy tapioca soup topped with coconut are refreshing counterpoints to the full-flavored dishes that usually precede them.

SWEET RICE WITH MANGOES

A day ahead, in a bowl, combine the rice and 6 cups (48 fl oz/1.5 l) water and let soak at room temperature overnight. Drain the rice once at the midway point and re-cover with 6 cups fresh water. The next day, pour water to a depth of 3 inches (7.5 cm) into a steamer pan. Line the steamer tray with a 20-inch (50-cm) square of cheesecloth (muslin). Drain the rice and spread in the lined tray. Place the tray in the steamer pan and set the steamer over high heat. Bring the water to a boil, drape the overhanging cheesecloth loosely over the rice, cover, and steam for 20 minutes. Remove the tray of rice from the steamer, and lift out the rice-filled cheesecloth packet. Reline the steamer tray with clean cheesecloth and invert the half-cooked rice back into the steamer tray. Drape the rice with the new cheesecloth, cover, and steam over high heat until the rice kernels are tender, about 20 minutes longer.

Meanwhile, to make sauce one, in a saucepan over low heat, combine the coconut milk, granulated sugar, and salt and bring to a low simmer, stirring to dissolve the sugar. To make sauce two, combine the coconut cream and palm sugar in a separate pan and warm over low heat, stirring to dissolve the sugar. Let both sauces cool to room temperature.

Line 6 small ramekins with 8-inch (20-cm) squares of plastic wrap. Transfer the rice to a bowl. Using a spatula, gradually mix in sauce one. Divide the rice among the ramekins, pressing down to distribute it evenly, and cover with the plastic wrap. Let stand at room temperature for at least 30 minutes or for up to 2 hours. Do not refrigerate. Place a banana leaf shape (if using) on a plate. Fold back the plastic wrap on each ramekin, and invert onto each leaf. Lift off the ramekin and peel off the plastic. Garnish with 3 or 4 mango slices, drizzle with 2 tablespoons of sauce two, and sprinkle with sesame seeds. Pass the remaining sauce at the table.

MAKES 6 SERVINGS

CUTTING BANANA LEAVES

In Southeast Asia, long, pliable banana leaves are used for wrapping foods before cooking to help keep the foods moist. The leaves are also used to create decorations for serving platters. Banana leaves are usually sold frozen. To use them for decoration, defrost them at room temperature, wipe them with a damp cloth, and use scissors to cut them into shapes such as stars, triangles, diamonds, or crescent moons. Place, shiny side up, on plates and rub lightly with canola oil.

1 cup (7 oz/220 g) glutinous rice (page 106)

FOR SAUCE ONE:

½ cup (4 fl oz/125 ml) coconut milk

¼ cup (2 oz/60 g) granulated sugar

2 pinches of salt

FOR SAUCE TWO:

1 cup (8 fl oz/250 ml) coconut cream (page 113)

½ cup (4 oz/125 g) chopped palm sugar (page 98) or brown sugar

24-inch (60-cm) piece banana leaf, wiped clean and cut into 6 decorative shapes (optional) (far left)

2 mangoes, peeled and sliced (page 114)

1 teaspoon sesame seeds, toasted (page 21)

TAPIOCA WITH COCONUT CREAM

1 cup (6 oz/185 g) small tapioca pearls *(far right)*

FOR THE SUGAR SYRUP:

¾ cup (6 oz/185 g) chopped palm sugar (page 98) or brown sugar

½ teaspoon vanilla extract (essence)

FOR THE COCONUT CREAM:

1 can (14 fl oz/430 ml) coconut milk

1½ teaspoons granulated sugar

2 pinches of salt

2 tablespoons unsweetened flaked dried coconut

In a large saucepan over high heat, bring 6 cups (48 fl oz/1.5 l) water to a boil. Add the tapioca pearls in a slow, steady stream, stirring constantly. Reduce the heat to low and simmer gently, uncovered, for 30 minutes, stirring frequently. The tapioca pearls will be undercooked with a white opaque center. Add 5 cups (40 fl oz/1.25 l) water to the tapioca and continue to simmer, uncovered, until the pearls are translucent throughout, about 30 minutes longer. Let cool to room temperature.

To make the sugar syrup, in a saucepan over medium heat, combine the palm sugar and 1 cup (8 fl oz/250 ml) water, and heat the mixture, stirring until the sugar dissolves and a syrup forms, about 5 minutes. Add the vanilla and continue to cook the syrup until it thickens enough to coat the back of a spoon, 7–10 minutes. Remove from the heat and let cool to room temperature.

To make the coconut cream, open the can of coconut milk without first shaking it. The milk in the can should be topped with a thick layer of cream. Scoop off enough cream from the can to measure about ½ cup (4 fl oz/125 ml) and pour it into a saucepan over low heat. Reserve the remaining coconut milk for another use. Whisk in the granulated sugar and salt, bring to a simmer, and simmer until the sugar dissolves, 2–3 minutes. Remove from the heat and let stand at room temperature.

Drain the tapioca in a fine-mesh sieve, then place the sieve of tapioca under a slow stream of cold water for 1 minute. Drain the tapioca of all the water and divide among individual bowls. Immediately drizzle with the sugar syrup, dividing it evenly, and then top with the coconut cream, dividing evenly. Garnish with the flaked coconut and serve at room temperature.

MAKES 6 SERVINGS

COOKING TAPIOCA

Tapioca flour, also known as tapioca starch, is a refined starch made from the tubers of the cassava plant. The same starch processed into bead form becomes tapioca pearls, off-white balls that range in size from a small seed to an English pea. Tapioca pearls are used in desserts, including this Thai pudding, sweet soups, and drinks, as well as some savory dishes. When cooked, they turn from opaque to translucent and have a thick, slightly gelatinous consistency. Do not use instant tapioca in place of pearl tapioca, as it will not yield the same result.

BANANA FRITTERS

To make the batter, in a bowl, sift together the all-purpose and rice flours, baking powder, and salt. Stir in the granulated sugar. Whisk in the coconut milk until the batter just comes together. Do not overstir. Cover and refrigerate for 30 minutes.

To make the filling, in a food processor, combine the peanuts, coconut, palm sugar, and salt and pulse until finely minced. Add the butter and pulse several times until the mixture has the consistency of cooked oatmeal.

If using large bananas, peel them and halve crosswise on the diagonal. If using small bananas, peel and leave whole. Place the bananas in a bowl and toss with the lime juice. Using a small, sharp knife, cut a lengthwise slit 3 inches (7.5 cm) long in each banana piece, forming a pocket. Using a butter knife, slip about 1 teaspoon of the filling into each pocket. Take care not to over-stuff the bananas.

Preheat the oven to 250°F (120°C). Line a baking sheet with a layer of paper towels.

Pour canola oil to a depth of 4 inches (10 cm) into a deep, heavy saucepan and heat to 375°F (190°C) on a deep-frying thermometer. When the oil is hot, dip 4 or 5 banana pieces into the batter, shake off the excess batter, and carefully slide the pieces into the oil. Fry until golden brown, 2–3 minutes. Using a skimmer, transfer the bananas to the paper towel–lined sheet to drain, and place in the oven to keep warm. Repeat with the remaining bananas, allowing the oil to reheat to 375°F before adding the next batch.

Divide the hot and crisp bananas among warmed individual plates. Using a fine-mesh sieve or a sifter, dust the bananas with confectioners' sugar and serve.

MAKES 4 SERVINGS

PALM SUGAR

In Southeast Asia, palm sugar, also known as coconut sugar, is a popular sweetener. It is made by boiling down the sap of a coconut palm, and is sold in a semisoft state in cans or in hard disks or cylinders. The sugar, ranging from a honey color to mahogany brown, has a rich caramel flavor. Brown sugar may be substituted, although the flavor will not be as complex or intense. If the palm sugar is too hard to spoon or cut with a knife, finely chop before measuring or use a handheld grater to shave off the desired amount.

FOR THE BATTER:

½ cup (2½ oz/75 g) all-purpose (plain) flour

½ cup (2 oz/60 g) rice flour

½ teaspoon baking powder

⅛ teaspoon salt

3 tablespoons granulated sugar

1 cup (8 fl oz/250 ml) coconut milk

FOR THE FILLING:

3 tablespoons unsalted peanuts, toasted (page 102) and minced

2 tablespoons unsweetened flaked dried coconut

2½ teaspoons grated palm sugar *(far left)* or brown sugar

2 pinches of salt

1 tablespoon unsalted butter

4 large, ripe bananas or 8 finger bananas

1 teaspoon fresh lime juice

Canola or peanut oil for deep-frying

Confectioners' (icing) sugar

SHAVED ICE WITH FRUIT AND RED BEANS

2½ cups (10 oz/315 g)
ice cubes

FOR THE SUGAR SYRUP:

⅓ cup (3 oz/90 g) sugar

FOR THE COCONUT CREAM:

1 can (14 fl oz/430 ml)
coconut milk

3 tablespoons unsweetened
condensed milk

¼ cup (1½ oz/45 g) diced
ripe mango (page 114) or
papaya (¼-inch/6-mm dice)

¼ cup (1 oz/30 g) diced
rinsed canned litchi
(¼-inch/6-mm dice)

¼ cup (1½ oz/45 g) diced
pineapple (¼-inch/6-mm
dice)

¼ cup (1 oz/30 g)
diced kiwifruit
(¼-inch/6-mm dice)

¼ cup (1½ oz/45 g) canned
sweetened azuki beans
(page 112), rinsed

1 tablespoon fresh
lime juice

In a food processor or sturdy blender, crush half of the ice cubes until snowlike in texture. Transfer to a large bowl. Repeat with the remaining ice cubes, add to the bowl, and place in the freezer until ready to use.

To make the sugar syrup, in a small saucepan over medium heat, combine the sugar and ½ cup (4 fl oz/125 ml) water and bring to a simmer, stirring to dissolve the sugar. Continue to simmer until a clear, thick syrup forms, 5–7 minutes. Remove from the heat, let cool, pour into a small pitcher, and refrigerate until ready to serve.

To make the coconut cream, open the can of coconut milk without first shaking it. The milk in the can should be topped with a thick layer of cream. Scoop off about ½ cup (4 fl oz/125 ml) cream and place in a small bowl. Reserve the remaining coconut milk for another use. Add the condensed milk and whisk together with the coconut cream until smooth. Cover and refrigerate until ready to serve.

In a bowl, combine the mango, litchi, pineapple, kiwifruit, and azuki beans. Add the lime juice and toss to coat.

Using an ice-cream scoop, mound a scoop of the crushed ice in each individual serving bowl. Spoon the fruit mixture over the ice, dividing it evenly. Drizzle the sugar syrup over the fruit, then spoon the coconut cream over the fruit, dividing both syrup and sauce evenly among the desserts. Serve at once.

MAKES 4–6 SERVINGS

LITCHI FRUIT

Native to southern China, the litchi fruit grows on an evergreen tree in bunches and looks like a large crimson berry with spiny, leathery skin. The peeled fruit reveals firm, white, semitranslucent flesh enclosing a dark, glossy seed. The taste of litchis is sweetly acid, much like a citrus fruit. Fresh litchis are available in markets only from midsummer to autumn; they are easily peeled and the seed removed. Canned litchis retain the fruits' flavor and texture surprisingly well, and are excellent in this refreshing Malaysian dessert. Rinse canned litchis of their sugar syrup before using.

GINGER-ALMOND SUGAR COOKIES

Preheat the oven to 375°F (190°C). Line 2 baking sheets with parchment (baking) paper.

In a bowl, whisk together the flour, ground almonds, baking powder, salt, and ground ginger, and set aside.

In a bowl, using a mixer set at medium speed, beat together the butter, 1 cup (8 oz/250 g) of the granulated sugar, and the brown sugar until light and fluffy, about 3 minutes. Add the 1 unbeaten egg, vanilla, and crystallized ginger and continue to beat at medium speed until combined, about 30 seconds. Reduce the speed to low, add the flour mixture, and beat just until combined.

Place the remaining ½ cup (4 oz/125 g) granulated sugar in a bowl. Fill a separate bowl with water. Dip your hands into the water and shake off the excess (this prevents the dough from sticking to your hands). Scoop up a tablespoon or so of dough and roll it between your palms into a ball 1½ inches (4 cm) in diameter. Roll the ball in the sugar, coating evenly, and place on a prepared baking sheet. Repeat with the remaining dough, moistening your hands after forming each ball and spacing the balls 2 inches (5 cm) apart on the baking sheet. Butter the bottom of a drinking glass, dip the bottom of the glass in the remaining sugar, and flatten the dough balls until they are ¾ inch (2 cm) thick. Brush the top of each flattened ball with the beaten egg, and then press a blanched almond into the center.

Bake the cookies until golden brown around the edges and very lightly colored in the center, 15–20 minutes. Let them cool on the baking sheets on wire racks for 3 minutes, then transfer the cookies to the racks and let cool to room temperature. The cookies should be crisp on the edges and chewy in the center. Store in an airtight container at room temperature for up to 1 week.

MAKES ABOUT 3 DOZEN COOKIES

TOASTING AND GRINDING NUTS

Almonds and other nuts are toasted to intensify their flavor. To toast almonds, preheat the oven to 375°F (190°C) and spread the nuts on a baking sheet. Toast until they are fragrant and have begun to color, about 10 minutes, then remove from the pan and let cool completely. For nuts with a higher oil content, such as pine nuts, cashews, and peanuts, reduce the toasting time to about 7 minutes. To grind toasted nuts, place them in a food processor and pulse to the desired consistency; do not overprocess, or the nuts will release oil and form a paste.

2 cups (10 oz/315 g) all-purpose (plain) flour

1 cup (5½ oz/170 g) unsalted almonds, toasted and finely ground *(far left)*

½ teaspoon baking powder

¼ teaspoon salt

⅛ teaspoon ground ginger

1 cup (8 oz/250 g) unsalted butter, softened

1½ cups (12 oz/375 g) granulated sugar

1 tablespoon light brown sugar

1 large egg, plus 1 beaten egg

1 teaspoon vanilla extract (essence)

3½ tablespoons finely minced crystallized ginger

36 unsalted blanched whole almonds

ASIAN BASICS

Every country in Asia, from Japan to India, boasts a unique national table. Yet these neighbors also reveal many culinary links in their use of equipment, their choice of ingredients, and their everyday cooking techniques.

SHARED TRADITIONS

Asian immigration to the West increased dramatically in the last decades of the twentieth century. The newcomers brought their native dishes with them, and now Chinese, Thai, Korean, Malaysian, Indonesian, Vietnamese, and Indian restaurants are common and popular around the world. Each cuisine has inspired its own distinctive identity, from the harmonious blend of color and texture in a Chinese stir-fry and the complex yet subtle spiciness in a Thai salad to the fiery heat of Indian curries and the simple elegance of Japanese tempura.

A careful blending of herbs and spices and an attention to complementary ingredients are just two of the characteristics common to all Asian cuisines. Once you try some of the flavor combinations in this book, you will want to share the dishes with your family and friends, as well.

EQUIPMENT

The wok, called by various local names, is the universal cooking pot of Asia. It is bowl shaped, with either a rounded bottom for using on a gas stove or a flat bottom for an electric stove. Its gently sloping slides are not only good heat conductors, but also effective barriers for foods that might escape during stir-frying. Woks are versatile, perfect utensils for stir-frying, deep-frying, steaming, and braising. They are available in carbon steel, stainless steel, aluminum, and nonstick finishes.

Stainless-steel or carbon-steel woks are recommended, as they are even conductors of heat. A 14-inch (35-cm) wok with a tight-fitting lid is ideal for preparing dishes for four to six people. If you are using a round-bottomed wok, you also need a hollow steel wok ring that sits directly over the gas burner. The wok rests securely in the ring, which holds it steady. In the absence of a wok, or if you cannot find a wok suited to an electric stove top, use a heavy-bottomed, deep, wide sauté pan.

Bamboo steamers, which come in various sizes, are constructed of circular bamboo frames with slat-bamboo bottoms and woven-bamboo-mesh lids. The most useful size is about 13 inches (33 cm) in diameter, which fits snugly in a 14-inch (35-cm) wok above the steaming water. Foods can be placed directly on the bamboo-slat base or on a plate or shallow bowl set on the base (page 58).

The mortar and pestle are ancient grinding tools that remain indispensable in the kitchens of Asia (page 10). They are used for grinding dried spices and seeds and for making complex chile pastes for dressings and curries. An electric coffee mill, reserved for spices only, is the quick and easy alternative for grinding toasted spices to the desired coarseness, just as a mini food processor is ideal for processing aromatic pastes.

A selection of high-quality, sharp knives is essential, with a good chef's knife the most important among them. This all-purpose cutting tool has a tapered blade and pointed tip and is available in various lengths. An 8-inch (20-cm) blade is suitable for most tasks. Use it for thinly slicing meat for such dishes as Korean Barbecued Beef (page 22), or for chopping or mincing chiles, shallots, garlic, cilantro, and other ingredients.

The flat side of the blade is handy for smashing lemongrass and ginger to break down their fibers, thereby releasing their flavor.

A sharpening steel will help you keep your knives well sharpened. Sharp blades are needed for accurate cutting and for safety. Stain-resistant high-carbon steel is the material of choice, as it holds an edge, will not discolor when it comes in contact with acidic foods, and will not rust.

Three additional tools will make your Asian cooking go more smoothly. A long-handled spatula with a shovel-shaped base, all stainless steel, is good for stir-frying. Its rounded edge fits the contour of the wok for lifting and tossing ingredients. (A wooden spatula or spoon can be substituted.) A wire skimmer, a round steel-mesh base attached to a long split-bamboo handle, is ideal for removing solid foods from liquids. (A long-handled, all-stainless-steel strainer with a round, perforated base is a good alternative.) A stainless-steel ladle, with a bowl 4 to 5 inches (10 to 13 cm) in diameter and a long handle, is valuable for serving soups and for efficiently scooping out solids and liquids together. For use with a nonstick wok, you will need a wooden spatula or tools made especially for nonstick cookware, to avoid scratching the wok's surface.

INGREDIENTS

Every Asian cuisine draws on some ingredients that are unique to it, but many of the same foods are found in kitchens throughout the region. Three ingredients that play central roles are rice, noodles, and tofu. For detailed information on other important Asian ingredients, see pages 112–15.

RICE

Rice has been a mainstay of the Asian diet for hundreds of generations. Most scholars believe that it is descended from a grass that grew wild in India in ancient times, and that its cultivation spread from the subcontinent first to China, then throughout Southeast Asia, and finally around the world. It is a filling starch and is present at almost every meal in Asia. Served with seafood, meats, poultry, and vegetables, rice provides a plain foil for rich and spicy dishes.

The rice most commonly eaten in Asia is long-grain white rice. Two highly prized long-grain types are basmati and jasmine. Basmati rice, widely cultivated in northern India, has long, slim kernels and a nutlike taste and aroma. Thai jasmine rice, which also has extra-long, slender grains, is named for its appealing floral scent and is appreciated beyond Thailand's borders. Glutinous rice,

sometimes called sweet rice or sticky rice, has shorter kernels and is high in amylose, a starch that makes the grains highly sticky when cooked.

In northern Thailand and Laos, glutinous rice is traditionally served alongside savory dishes; elsewhere it is more commonly used in savory and sweet dishes. Long-grain rice is most often cooked by the absorption method (page 61), while glutinous rice is usually steamed.

The photograph on pages 52–53 shows, from left to right, long-grain, glutinous, and basmati rice.

NOODLES

In the Asian diet, noodles are second in importance only to rice. Made from a variety of grains and legumes, they are enjoyed as a filling snack, a side dish, or sometimes a one-dish meal. Noodles are sold in a wide selection of shapes and sizes; can be fried, braised, boiled, or added to soups; and are served both hot and cold.

Shopping for noodles can be confusing because more than one name is often used for the same noodle. The key to identification is not the name on the package label, but its contents and knowing what the noodle should look like. The following are among the most commonly used noodles in Asian dishes.

Long, round, pale yellow Chinese egg noodles are available fresh or dried and thin (about the size of capellini) to thick (about the size of spaghetti). Made from wheat flour, water, and eggs, these all-purpose noodles can be stir-fried, pan-seared, braised, or stirred into a soup. If you cannot find good-quality Chinese egg noodles, substitute fresh or dried Italian pasta.

Dried rice noodles, labeled "rice sticks" (usually when flat) or "rice vermicelli" (usually when round), come in various widths, from threadlike strands to wide ribbons (about ¼ inch/ 6 mm). They must be reconstituted in hot water for at least 15 minutes until soft before using in a recipe. The exception is when they are deep-fried, usually for a garnish; the noodles expand several times their size within seconds of being put into hot oil. Fresh rice noodles are generally flat and about ½ inch (12 mm) wide. You can also buy rice noodle sheets and cut them into the desired width. Fresh noodles need only a quick rinse before cooking. Place them in a pot of just boiled water for 2 seconds and then drain immediately.

Cellophane noodles are dried noodles made from the starch of mung beans. Also known as bean threads, they are translucent in dried form and transparent after softening in hot water for 15 minutes. The softened noodles can be added to dishes without further cooking. When put into braised dishes or used in salads, they absorb the flavors of other ingredients. Like dried rice noodles, cellophane noodles can be deep-fried and used as a garnish.

Udon are white, wide Japanese noodles made from a dough of wheat flour and water. Sold fresh or dried and either round or flat, they are predominantly served in broth, in casseroles, or panfried.

Available dried or fresh, soba are brownish, thin Japanese noodles made from a dough of buckwheat flour, usually a smaller amount of wheat flour, and water. Nutty in flavor and rich in protein and fiber, they are served cold with a dipping sauce or hot in soups.

The photograph on pages 66–67 shows, clockwise from top left, egg, cellophane, and soba noodles.

TOFU

First made in China, tofu, also known as bean curd, is a high-protein, custardlike product made from soybeans. Dried beans are softened in water, crushed, boiled, and finally strained to separate the liquid, or milk, from the pulp. A coagulant is added to the milk to separate the curds from the whey, then the curds are strained and pressed to make soft pillows or firm blocks. The texture of tofu ranges from silken to extra firm, and the type used is chosen according to the dish being prepared. Fresh tofu readily absorbs flavors from surrounding foods or sauces and marries well with a variety of ingredients. Store covered with water in the refrigerator for up to 5 days, changing the water daily.

For soft tofu, the curds are pressed only lightly to form a cake. The result is a particularly delicate texture for using in mild soups and braised dishes.

More fully pressed firm tofu is easier to work with than soft tofu because it is less likely to break up in handling. It may be poached and tossed in a salad and can up stand to stir-frying. The firmer the tofu, the more readily it absorbs other flavors, making firm tofu a good choice for dishes prepared with a rich sauce or complex seasonings.

Extra-firm tofu, the firmest tofu, is achieved by heavy pressing of the curds. It is sturdy and dense, making it a good textural substitute for meat. Like firm tofu, it soaks up flavors readily and is a good choice for stir-fried and braised dishes.

Deep-fried tofu is made by deep-frying pieces of soft tofu until the surface is crisp and golden brown and the inside is soft and white. Used primarily in vegetarian cooking, it is often braised with strong seasonings. Look for deep-fried tofu in plastic bags in the refrigerated section; use it within 3 days of purchase.

COOKING TECHNIQUES

As with ingredients, certain cooking techniques are common to all Asian cuisines, and mastering them is important to turning out successful meals. Two of the most popular, deep-frying and stir-frying, share two basic characteristics: they cook foods quickly and can be done in a wok.

DEEP-FRYING

Deep-frying is widely used in Asia both for savory dishes, such as Vegetable and Shrimp Tempura (page 29), and sweet dishes, such as Banana Fritters (page 98). When correctly deep-fried, foods will have a crisp, tender, golden crust and a fully cooked interior. If using a round-bottomed wok, be sure to use a wok ring to ensure that the pan does not tip during frying. In the absence of a wok, use any heavy-bottomed, deep, wide pan. Also, always use oil that has a high smoke point (the temperature to which it can be heated before it begins to smoke). Canola and peanut oil are two good choices.

Fill the pan with oil to a depth of 4–5 inches (10–13 cm), place over high heat, and heat until the oil registers 375°F (190°C) on a deep-frying thermometer, or to the temperature indicated in the recipe. Carefully slide the food into the hot oil, slipping it in at the edges of the pan, rather than at the center. Cook the food in small batches; if you add too much to the oil at once, the temperature will drop dramatically and the food will absorb the oil. Adjust the heat as needed to keep the oil temperature steady, and use a wire skimmer or a slotted spoon to turn and separate the pieces as they cook. When the food is ready, still using the skimmer or spoon, transfer it to paper towels to drain, then skim any bits of food or batter from the oil. Always wait for the oil to return to frying temperature before adding the next batch.

STIR-FRYING

Stir-frying preserves the fresh flavor, color, and texture of ingredients by rapidly frying small pieces of food in oil over high heat as they are stirred constantly to ensure even cooking. It is a quick process, so careful planning and execution are critical. Have everything you need, tools and ingredients alike, close at hand before you begin cooking, including warmed plates or bowls for serving. Allow time for the wok to heat fully, and then carefully coat the pan with oil before adding the ingredients. Once the ingredients are in the wok, toss and stir them vigorously for quick, even cooking.

1 **Assembling the ingredients**: Make sure everything is ready before you begin heating the wok. This includes cutting all ingredients into uniform pieces; marinating the meat, if using; mixing any sauce ingredients in a bowl; and preparing any garnishes.

2 **Heating the wok and the oil**: To ensure even heating and to prevent foods from sticking to the pan, heat an empty wok over high heat until very hot, 30–40 seconds. Add oil (use one with a high smoke point such as canola or peanut oil) and swirl the pan to coat the bottom and the sides evenly. Alternatively, use a metal or wooden spatula or spoon to spread the oil over the bottom and sides. Allow the oil to heat to near smoking.

3 **Adding the ingredients**: First, add the aromatics, usually garlic and ginger, and stir-fry for several seconds until fragrant. Then add the ingredients requiring the longest cooking, such as dense vegetables or meat, followed by quicker-cooking items. Stir and toss the food vigorously until cooked.

4 **Adding the sauce**: If the recipe calls for a sauce, quickly stir it, pour into the wok, stir to combine with the other ingredients, and cook until lightly thickened. Quickly transfer to a platter, plates, or bowls, garnish, and serve.

BASIC RECIPES

Following are recipes for spicy, refreshing, and flavorful dipping sauces, chutneys, and other accompaniments, to enhance or serve alongside the recipes in this book.

GINGER-SOY DIPPING SAUCE

5 tablespoons (2½ fl oz/75 ml) rice vinegar

¼ cup (2 fl oz/60 ml) light soy sauce

2 tablespoons dark soy sauce

3 tablespoons warm water

1½ tablespoons sugar

1 tablespoon Asian sesame oil

1 teaspoon Sriracha chile sauce (page 115)

2 tablespoons peeled and minced fresh ginger

2 teaspoons minced garlic

2 teaspoons red jalapeño chile or other fresh hot red chile, seeded and thinly sliced on the diagonal

In a small, nonaluminum bowl, whisk together the vinegar, light and dark soy sauces, warm water, sugar, sesame oil, and chile sauce until the sugar dissolves. Stir in the ginger, garlic, and chile. Use immediately, or cover and refrigerate for up to 2 days. Makes about 1¼ cups (10 fl oz/310 ml).

Serving Tip: Offer the dipping sauce with Pot Stickers (page 17) and noodle dishes.

RAITA

½ cup (2½ oz/75 g) peeled, seeded, and minced cucumber

1½ teaspoons salt, plus salt to taste

2 cloves garlic, minced

1 cup (8 oz/250 g) low-fat plain yogurt

2 tablespoons fresh lemon juice

½ teaspoon ground cumin

⅛ teaspoon ground white pepper, plus pepper to taste

2 tablespoons minced fresh cilantro (fresh coriander)

Place the cucumber in a sieve, toss with 1 teaspoon of the salt, place over a bowl, and let drain for 30 minutes. Pat the cucumber dry with paper towels.

In a mortar, combine the garlic and the remaining ½ teaspoon salt and grind together with a pestle until a paste forms. Alternatively, combine the ingredients on a plastic cutting board and mash together with a knife to form a paste. In a bowl, combine the cucumber and the garlic paste with the yogurt, lemon juice, cumin, white pepper, and cilantro and stir to mix. Taste and adjust the seasoning with salt and white pepper. Use immediately, or cover and refrigerate for up to 2 days. Makes 1½ cups (12 fl oz/375 ml).

Serving Tip: Serve raita with Lamb Biryani (page 57) and as an accompaniment to other Indian rice and curry dishes.

CHILE SAMBAL

8 red jalapeño chiles or other fresh hot red chiles, seeded and chopped

4 shallots, chopped

6 cloves garlic, chopped

1 teaspoon sugar

½ teaspoon salt

3 tablespoons canola or peanut oil

½ teaspoon shrimp paste (page 114)

1 tablespoon fresh lime juice

In a mortar, combine the chiles, shallots, garlic, sugar, and salt and grind with a pestle until a paste forms. Add 1–2 tablespoons water if needed to facilitate grinding.

In a small frying pan over high heat, heat the canola oil. Add the chile paste and sauté for several minutes until the paste is fragrant. Reduce the heat to medium, stir in the shrimp paste and lime juice, and continue to sauté until the mixture thickens, 7–10 minutes. Transfer to a bowl and let cool to room temperature. Use immediately or cover and refrigerate for up to 2 weeks. Makes ½ cup (4 fl oz/125 ml).

Serving Tip: The chile sambal can be passed at the table and used to add flavor and heat to such dishes as Indonesian Spicy Chicken Noodle Soup (page 48), Malaysian Spicy Fried Rice with Shrimp (page 61), and Malaysian Stir-Fried Noodles with Beef (page 75).

CILANTRO AND MINT CHUTNEY

2 cups (2 oz/30 g) fresh cilantro (fresh coriander) leaves

½ cup (½ oz/15 g) fresh mint leaves

1 green serrano chile, seeded and chopped

1 green (spring) onion, chopped

1 tablespoon peeled and grated fresh ginger

1 clove garlic, minced

2 tablespoons unsalted peanuts, toasted (page 102) and chopped

1 teaspoon cumin seeds, toasted and ground (page 21)

½ teaspoon salt

¼ teaspoon sugar

⅛ teaspoon ground black pepper

¼ cup (2 fl oz/60 ml) fresh lemon juice

In a mortar, combine the cilantro, mint, chile, green onion, ginger, garlic, peanuts, cumin, salt, sugar, and black pepper and grind together with a pestle until a thick paste forms. Add 1–2 tablespoons water if needed to facilitate grinding. Alternatively, combine the ingredients in a mini food processor and process to a thick paste. Pour into a bowl and stir in the lemon juice and ¼ cup (2 fl oz/60 ml) water. Use immediately, or cover and refrigerate for up to 4 days. Makes 1½ cups (12 fl oz/375 ml).

Serving Tip: Serve the chutney with Lamb Biryani (page 57) and as an accompaniment to other Indian rice and curry dishes.

TAMARIND CHUTNEY

½ cup (4 oz/125 g) tamarind concentrate (page 115)

5 tablespoons (2½ oz/75 g) sugar

1 teaspoon peeled and grated fresh ginger

1½ teaspoons cumin seeds, toasted and ground (page 21)

½ teaspoon salt

⅛ teaspoon ground cayenne pepper

½ teaspoon fresh lemon juice

In a saucepan over low heat, combine the tamarind concentrate, sugar, and ¾ cup (6 fl oz/180 ml) water, bring to a simmer, and stir until the sugar dissolves, about 3 minutes. Add the ginger, cumin, salt, cayenne, and lemon juice, stir well, and continue to simmer over low heat for 5 minutes longer to blend the flavors.

Remove from the heat and let cool to room temperature. Use immediately, or cover and refrigerate for up to 1 week. Makes 1 cup (8 fl oz/250 ml).

Serving Tip: Serve the chutney with Vegetable Samosas (page 33) and grilled meats

NUOC CHAM

3 cloves garlic, chopped

1½ tablespoons sugar

3 tablespoons fish sauce

2 tablespoons rice vinegar

2 tablespoons fresh lime juice

1 serrano chile, seeded and thinly sliced on the diagonal

1 tablespoon grated carrot

1 tablespoon grated daikon

Using a mortar and pestle, grind together the garlic and sugar until a paste forms. Alternatively, combine the ingredients in a mini food processor and process to a paste. Transfer to a bowl and whisk in the fish sauce, rice vinegar, lime juice, and ¼ cup (2 fl oz/60 ml) water. Pour through a fine-mesh sieve into a clean bowl and add the chile, carrot, and daikon. Makes about ⅔ cup (5 fl oz/160 ml).

Serving Tip: Nuoc cham is a condiment offered as an accompaniment to myriad Vietnamese dishes, including summer rolls (page 26), crêpes (page 37), beef noodle soup (page 44), and grilled chicken with noodles (page 68).

GLOSSARY

Many areas in Western countries are home to growing Asian communities and have ethnic grocery stores or mainstream supermarkets that cater to a diversity of customers and cooking styles. But even if you do not live in an area where Asian groceries are readily available, you can look to specialty-food stores, mail-order retailers, and the Internet as excellent sources of the ingredients used in authentic Asian cooking.

ASIAN SESAME OIL A dark amber oil pressed from toasted white sesame seeds, Asian sesame oil has a distinctive nutty aroma and taste. Unlike other oils used for cooking, sesame oil is added in small amounts as a flavoring agent to marinades and dressings or to soups and braised or stir-fried dishes during the final minutes of cooking.

AZUKI BEANS Small dried azuki beans, also known as adzuki beans or red beans, are soaked, boiled, and sweetened with sugar before canning. Used primarily in Asian desserts, the sweetened beans are added whole to sweet soups and coconut milk drinks and are spooned on shaved ice. When using the beans whole in a recipe, place in a fine-mesh sieve and rinse briefly to remove excess syrup.

BONITO FLAKES These delicate, buff-colored, almost translucent flakes are shaved from a bonito fish that has been dried and smoked. The shavings have a subtle fish taste and aroma, and are one of the principal ingredients in dipping sauces and bonito stock, or *dashi* (page 14), a traditional Japanese fish stock. Bonito flakes are also sprinkled on cooked vegetables and fried dishes as a garnish. To keep the flakes fresh, store them in a sealed container in a cool, dry place.

CHILES
Fresh and dried chiles are important ingredients in the cuisines of many regions of China and Southeast Asia. With most chile varieties, the smaller and greener the chile, the hotter its flesh will be. Red chiles are ripe versions of green chiles. To reduce the heat of fresh chiles, carefully cut out the ribs, or membranes, and discard the seeds (page 82).

Jalapeño: Broad-shouldered chile 3–4 inches (7.5–10 cm) long. Available green or red, jalapeños are good all-purpose full-flavored chiles that range from mildly hot to fiery. Red, or ripe, jalapeños are less common than green jalapeños in food stores; red serrano chiles may be substituted.

Serrano: Smooth-skinned, cylindrical chile 2–3 inches (5–7.5 cm) long. Serranos, available green or red, tend to carry more heat than jalapeños.

Thai: Small red or green chile averaging 1 inch (2.5 cm) in length. Also known as bird or bird's-eye chiles, Thai chiles are stronger in flavor than other chiles and are among the hottest fresh chiles used in Asian cooking. To add extra heat to a dish, substitute Thai chiles for jalapeños or serranos.

CHINESE RICE WINE Rich amber in color with a full-bodied bouquet, Chinese rice wine is the product of fermented glutinous rice and millet that is aged for a minimum of 10 years. The wine is similar to dry sherry in flavor and aroma, and can be served warm or cold as a beverage. It is also used in cooking, primarily in marinades and sauces. The best-quality rice wine is from eastern China and is named after the province of Shaoxing.

CILANTRO See page 68.

CLARIFIED BUTTER This form of butter is obtained by simmering butter until the water evaporates, then pouring off and preserving the liquid that separates from the milk solids. Used predominantly in Indian cooking and known as *ghee,* it contributes a rich buttery taste to food, is much less perishable than butter, and is an ideal medium for frying, due to its high smoke point.

To make clarified butter, melt 1 cup (8 oz/250 g) unsalted butter in a small saucepan over low heat. Simmer the butter, without stirring, until the white milk solids settle to the bottom of the pan and begin to brown, about 20 minutes. Carefully skim off and discard any foam on top of the melted butter. Remove from the heat, let cool slightly, and pour the clear liquid through a fine-mesh sieve into a glass container, leaving the white milk solids behind. Discard the solids. Cover and refrigerate for up to 3 months.

COCONUT MILK AND CREAM
Despite its name, coconut milk is not a dairy product but is made by processing unsweetened grated coconut and water. This essential ingredient in Southeast Asian cooking is used in a broad range of dishes from soups and sauces to curries to desserts. Before opening a can of coconut milk, shake it well to blend the milk and cream. If a recipe calls for coconut cream, open the can without shaking it and spoon the thick layer of cream from the top. The liquid remaining in the can is thin coconut milk.

CUCUMBERS, PEELING AND SEEDING
Peeling the skin from cucumbers is recommended if the skin has been waxed or if it has a bitter taste. When using cucumbers in salads or other dishes, the seeds are removed as well.

To peel a cucumber, use a swivel-bladed vegetable peeler. To seed the cucumber, slice it in half lengthwise. Use a melon baller or spoon to scoop out the seeds and surrounding pulpy matter.

EGGS, HARD-BOILED Some Asian dishes, including Indonesian Spicy Chicken Noodle Soup (page 48) and Lamb Biryani (page 57), are garnished with hard-boiled eggs. It is easy to over-cook hard-boiled eggs, which results in yolks with an unsightly greenish tinge and a dry texture.

To make hard-boiled eggs, put the eggs in a saucepan and add cold water to cover them by 2 inches (5 cm). Bring to a boil over medium heat. When the water begins to boil, remove from the heat, cover, and let the eggs stand in the water for 20 minutes. Rinse under cold running water until cool, then peel.

EGGS, RAW Eggs are sometimes used raw or partially cooked in some Asian recipes, including Udon with Tofu and Egg (page 14). These eggs run a risk of being infected with salmonella or other bacteria, which can lead to food poisoning. This risk is of most concern to small children, older people, pregnant women, and anyone with a compromised immune system. If you have health and safety concerns, do not eat raw eggs.

ENOKI MUSHROOMS Delicately flavored enoki grow in small clumps and have small white caps and slender stems 2–3 inches (5–7.5 cm) long. Their mild flavor and smooth texture make the mushrooms suitable for use as an ingredient or a garnish for salads, clear soups, and braised dishes.

FINGER BANANA This variety of small banana ranges from yellow to red in color and grows in tight bunches shaped like hands. Firm in texture and creamy in consistency, finger bananas are used in such desserts as soups with coconut milk and puddings of sticky rice. In parts of Southeast Asia, they are grilled or are dipped in batter and fried.

FISH SAUCE See page 72.

GALANGAL Also known as Thai ginger, and used as well in the kitchens of Cambodia, Laos, and Indonesia, this cream-colored rhizome with thin black rings and pink shoots has a distinctive hot, peppery taste and a coarse texture. Peel it with a vegetable peeler or paring knife before using.

GINGER See page 54.

HOISIN SAUCE This sweet, tangy, reddish brown sauce is made from fermented soybeans, vinegar, sugar, garlic, and spices. The versatile sauce is used to flavor meat dishes, is added to dipping sauces, and is offered at the table as a condiment. Hoisin sauce is sold in jars and will keep indefinitely stored in the refrigerator.

KIMCHI Cabbage is fermented with chile sauce, garlic, ginger, salt, and other seasonings to make a spicy, pungent condiment that is enjoyed with Korean dishes such as barbecued beef (page 22). The cabbage is marinated for at least 24 hours before serving, and the longer it marinates, the stronger the flavor. Kimchi is sold in plastic tubs or jars.

MADRAS CURRY POWDER Originally from south India, this mixture of ground spices is used mainly in Southeast Asian cooking for seasoning curries, coconut-based soups, meats, and vegetables. The mildly spicy, aromatic powder usually consists of turmeric, cumin, coriander, cinnamon, cardamom, and black peppercorns. Store curry powder in a cool, dry place. Like other spices and dried herbs, it can lose potency after 2 months and may need to be replaced.

MANGO First grown in India and now widely cultivated in Southeast Asia, this fragrant, oval-shaped fruit has skin that ranges from green to pale yellow or orange. The light to deep yellow flesh is sweet, juicy, and aromatic. Soft, ripe mangoes are enjoyed in desserts. When hard and unripe, they are shredded for use in salads or for pickling.

To slice a mango, first peel it. Then stand it on a narrow side on a cutting board. Using a sharp knife and positioning it slightly off-center, cut all the flesh from one side of the pit in a single piece. Place each mango half cut side down and cut lengthwise into thin slices ¼ inch (6 mm) wide. Trim off the flesh encircling the pit.

MIRIN An important ingredient in Japanese cuisine, *mirin* is a sweet cooking wine made by fermenting glutinous rice and sugar. The pale gold and syrupy wine adds a rich flavor and translucent sheen to sauces, dressings, grilled meats, and simmered dishes.

MUNG BEAN SPROUTS These delicate sprouts with a refreshing, slightly crunchy texture are excellent in soups, salads, and stir-fried dishes. About 2 inches (5 cm) long, they have yellow-green heads and silvery white stems. Mung bean sprouts are best eaten fresh or added close to the end of cooking to preserve their crisp texture. These highly perishable sprouts are best purchased in bulk and will keep, stored in an airtight container, for up to 3 days.

NONALUMINUM Selecting cookware made from a nonreactive material such as stainless steel, enamel, or glass is important when cooking with acidic ingredients such as citrus juice, vinegar, wine, tomatoes, and most vegetables. Cookware made with materials such as aluminum (and, to a lesser degree, cast iron or unlined copper) will react with acidic ingredients and may impart a metallic taste and grayish color.

OYSTER SAUCE See page 18.

RICE FLOUR Raw long-grain rice is ground to produce a flour that is used for making rice noodles and rice paper and as an ingredient in batters for crêpes, fritters, and steamed cakes. This type of rice flour should not be confused with glutinous rice flour, which is made from short-grain glutinous rice and is used for making dumplings and desserts with a chewy consistency.

RICE PAPER See page 26.

RICE VINEGAR Popular in Chinese and Japanese cooking, rice vinegar is a clear, mild, and slightly sweet vinegar produced from fermented glutinous rice. It is an essential seasoning for salad dressings, soups, and sauces, and for making a brine for pickling. Rice vinegar is available plain or sweetened; the latter is marketed as seasoned rice vinegar.

SHICHIMI This Japanese condiment consists of ground red chile and other seasonings, including sesame seeds and black pepper. Small jars of shichimi are placed on the tables of Japanese restaurants for diners to sprinkle the mildly spicy seasoning on soups, noodles, and other dishes.

SHIITAKE MUSHROOMS Ranging from buff to dark brown in color, fresh shiitake mushrooms have smooth, plump caps and sturdy stems that should be trimmed and discarded. The mushrooms are also available dried and are often sold as dried Chinese black mushrooms. The dried mushrooms must be reconstituted in boiling water before using in a recipe (see page 30).

SHRIMP PASTE This seasoning indispensable to authentic Southeast Asian cooking is made from ground, salted, and fermented shrimp. The pale purple or pink paste has a very pungent aroma and an intense taste that diminishes when the paste is added to a sauce, curry, or other cooked dish. Shrimp paste is available in jars and tubs and in brick form. Because of its strong aroma, the paste should be stored in a tightly sealed container in the refrigerator.

SHRIMP, PEELING AND DEVEINING

Shrimp are often shelled and deveined before they are cooked. If a shrimp still has its head, pull it off or cut it off with a knife. Carefully pull off the legs on the shrimp's inside curve. Peel off the shell, beginning at the head end of the shrimp. Pull off the tail unless the recipe calls for it to be left attached.

Some shrimp have a dark intestinal vein that is removed primarily for aesthetic reasons. Using a paring knife, make a shallow cut following the curve of the shrimp's back just down to the vein. Slip the tip of the knife under the vein, lift it, pull it away, and rinse the shrimp under running cold water.

SOY SAUCE

A mixture of soybeans, wheat, and water is fermented to make this thin, dark, salty sauce. Of the various types of soy sauce available, the following are used in this book.

Dark soy: Less salty than light soy, and also thicker, darker, and sweeter due to the addition of molasses. Often used in combination with light soy sauce, dark soy sauce is added to marinades and slow-cooked dishes, and is used as a glaze for grilled meats.

Light soy: Salty, yet subtle sauce traditionally used in marinades, stir-fry sauces, and salad dressings, and also served as a dipping sauce.

Sweet soy: Dark, sweet, syrupy sauce popular mainly in Southeast Asian cooking. This variety is sweetened with palm sugar and typically seasoned with star anise and garlic. It is used for flavoring cooked foods and as a table condiment.

SRIRACHA CHILE SAUCE

Originating in southern Thailand, this general-purpose sauce is used sparingly to add zest to salads, noodle soups, and a wide range of other cooked dishes. It is also a table condiment offered at many Southeast Asian restaurants. The bright red-orange sauce is a mixture of ground chiles, tomatoes, vinegar, garlic, salt, and sugar.

STAR ANISE

Star anise is the dried seedpod of a Chinese tree related to the magnolia. Used in many Asian cuisines, the star-shaped pod has a distinct spiced licorice flavor that complements meat stews, braised vegetables, rice dishes, and other simmered dishes. When using whole star anise in a recipe, be sure to remove it before serving.

TAMARIND CONCENTRATE

Sold in jars, this thick sauce is derived from the sticky brown pulp inside the pods from tamarind trees. The concentrate adds a sweet-and-sour flavor to curries, chutneys, soups, and dipping sauces. Jars of the concentrate should be refrigerated after opening.

THAI BASIL See page 34.

WASABI PASTE A uniquely Japanese ingredient, fiery hot, light green wasabi paste is the classic condiment for sushi, sashimi, and cold soba noodles. Genuine wasabi paste is made by grating the root of the wasabi plant, an ingredient that is difficult to find outside Japan. Prepared wasabi paste, sold in tubes, is a good substitute. Powdered wasabi, packaged in small cans, can be used in place of the prepared paste. To reconstitute powdered wasabi, spoon some of the powder into a small bowl and add enough lukewarm water to make a fairly dense paste, stirring well to blend.

WATER CHESTNUTS Fresh water chestnuts are walnut-sized, dark brown tubers grown in ponds, streams, and rivers. The white flesh inside this vegetable is sweet and slightly starchy and has a crunchy texture. Fresh water chestnuts are sold in Asian markets and should be peeled before use. Easier to find are canned water chestnuts, which do not need to be peeled but should be rinsed.

WHITE MISO PASTE Protein-rich miso paste consists of fermented soybeans combined with barley, rice, or wheat. There are several types of miso, which are defined by the type of grain used. White miso, or *shiro miso*, made from soybeans and rice, is pale yellow and has a mild flavor. Its subtly sweet taste is appreciated in many Japanese soups, sauces, and marinades for seafood and vegetables.

INDEX

SIMON & SCHUSTER SOURCE
A Division of Simon & Schuster, Inc.
Rockefeller Center
1230 Avenue of the Americas
New York, NY 10020

WILLIAMS-SONOMA
Founder and Vice-Chairman: Chuck Williams

WELDON OWEN INC.
Chief Executive Officer: John Owen
President: Terry Newell
Chief Operating Officer: Larry Partington
Vice President, International Sales: Stuart Laurence
Creative Director: Gaye Allen
Series Editor: Sarah Putman Clegg
Managing Editor: Judith Dunham
Editor: Heather Belt
Designer: Teri Gardiner
Production Director: Chris Hemesath
Color Manager: Teri Bell
Shipping and Production Coordinator: Libby Temple

Weldon Owen wishes to thank the following
people for their generous assistance and support
in producing this book: Copy Editor Sharon Silva;
Food Stylists Kim Konecny and Erin Quon;
Photographer's Assistant Faiza Ali; Proofreaders
Arin Hailey and Desne Ahlers; Production Designer
Linda Bouchard; and Indexer Ken DellaPenta.

Set in Trajan, Utopia, and Vectora.

Williams-Sonoma Collection *Asian* was
conceived and produced by Weldon Owen Inc.,
814 Montgomery Street, San Francisco,
California 94133, in collaboration with
Williams-Sonoma, 3250 Van Ness Avenue,
San Francisco, California 94109.

A Weldon Owen Production
Copyright © 2003 by Weldon Owen Inc. and
Williams-Sonoma Inc.

SIMON & SCHUSTER SOURCE and colophon are
registered trademarks of Simon & Schuster, Inc.

For information regarding special discounts for
bulk purchases, please contact Simon & Schuster
Special Sales at 1-800-456-6798 or
business@simonandschuster.com

Color separations by Bright Arts Graphics
Singapore (Pte.) Ltd.
Printed and bound in Singapore by Tien Wah
Press (Pte.) Ltd.

First printed in 2003.

10 9 8 7 6 5 4 3 2 1

Library of Congress Cataloging-in-Publication
data is available.

ISBN 0-7432-5333-7

A NOTE ON WEIGHTS AND MEASURES

All recipes include customary U.S. and metric measurements. Metric conversions are based on
a standard developed for these books and have been rounded off. Actual weights may vary.